# KARL MARX
## in London

Published by The Langley Press, 2023

# KARL
# MARX
## in London

by

Simon Webb

Also from the Langley Press

Joe Hill: Life and Death of an American Rebel

Ignatius Sancho: An African in Eighteenth-Century London

John Lilburne: Gentleman, Leveller, Quaker

Galaxy Man: Thomas Wright of Durham

Lives of Famous Dwarfs

1889-1895: The First Coronavirus Pandemic?

For more Langley Press books, please visit our website at
www.langleypress.co.uk

# Contents

The modern Great Court of the British Museum, with the reading room at its centre (picture by Andrew Dunn)

# The British Museum Reading Room

*Some of these days, the Terrors of the Reading Room*
*of the British Museum will be written*

Edward Aveling, 1883

In a memorable episode in David Lodge's 1965 novel *The British Museum is Falling Down*, the hero, a scholar called Adam Appleby, returns to his desk to find that his books and papers have been moved, and that three men from communist China are examining the desk very closely. Appleby has been having a strange morning, plagued with hallucinations, and the appearance of the three mysterious Chinese men just heightens his feeling that his life is both inexplicable and beyond his control.

Appleby's desk is in the old reading room of the British Museum in London's Bloomsbury, and the Chinese men are part of a delegation that is being shown around the place. They are gazing reverentially at Appleby's desk because it is supposed to be the one used a century earlier by Karl Marx, the founder of Marxism and the father of communism, and therefore a historical personage of particular interest to visitors from Mao Zedong's China. Marx used the reading room every day for nearly thirty years, but according to Marjorie Caygill's 2000 book on the room, it is impossible to say exactly which of the desks Marx favoured.

Other past users of the reading room who would surely have been of interest to the communist Chinese would have been the Chinese nationalist leader Sun Yat-sen, and Vladimir Lenin, who signed in under the alias Jacob Richter (the enthusiastic use of aliases by Russian revolutionaries is one factor that makes it hard to work out exactly what many of them actually did while they were in England).

David Lodge mentions how his Chinese men wear 'loose, belted uniforms of some drab, coarse-grained material'. Lodge was probably imagining a winter version of the once-ubiquitous uniform of the communist Chinese, now known as a Mao Suit, but actually introduced under the aforementioned Sun Yat-sen.

In Max Beerbohm's 1916 story *Enoch Soames*, set in 1897, the eponymous hero is projected forward a century to visit the British Museum reading room in 1997. Here he finds that everyone working in the room looks pretty much the same: they are all dressed in 'sanitary woollen' of a 'greyish-yellowish' colour. It also transpires that the spelling of English has been reformed to make it more phonetic, and that all literature is now created under the wing of the state. This is pretty much like China under Mao, with its drab civilian uniforms, state control of everything, and language reforms. By 1997, however, the economic reforms introduced by Deng Xiaoping meant that the Chinese under Jiang Zemin had a more varied, western look than they had had under Mao.

The prospect that the 'levelling up' that it was thought would follow the introduction of a communist system of government might lead to a tedious blandness and sameness in everything has often been held up as an objection to such a system. Marx's distant relative and Paris friend the German poet Heinrich Heine expressed his fears about the possible coarsening of European culture under communism, in 1855. In the introduction to the French edition of his *Lutetia*, a book of articles he sent from Paris to the German newspaper the *Augsburger Zeitung*, he expressed his belief that the communists would inevitable take over Europe, but called them 'gloomy iconoclasts' with 'heavy hands' who would plant potatoes where laurels used to grow (poets were traditionally crowned with wreaths of laurel).

As well as Marx, Sun Yat-sen and Lenin, the list of past users of the British Museum reading room includes Oscar Wilde, Marcus Garvey and Virginia Woolf. The room functioned as a reference library – that is to say, users could consult the books and other items, but not borrow them. And they could only seek out their own books to a limited extent: they were supposed to consult the volumes of the catalogue (which had their own shelves in the reading room) and then arrange for items to be brought to them, rather as a duke might ask his butler to bring up a bottle or two from the cellar.

Despite decades of merciless government cuts, such reference libraries still exist all over the UK, and those based in public libraries can be used by pretty much anyone without charge. In Marx's day, the British Museum reading room didn't let in just anybody. Would-be users had to apply for a ticket: many were turned down, and some temporary tickets were not renewed. It seems not to have been the case that people were given access on the basis of nationality or social class. Edward Aveling, of whom more later, wrote about dirty people in the reading room, and far too many descriptions of the place from the Victorian period use the word 'hunger'. Here, it seems, people who were too poor to wash or feed themselves properly could still use books to distract themselves from their predicament.

To judge from some stories and indeed cartoons that feature in Marjorie Caygill's book *The British Museum Reading Room*, published by the Trustees of the BM in 2000, the guardians of the reading room, who would allow in the dirty and the hungry, did not only allow in people who were pursuing some credible course of study. Some just used the room as a warm, quiet place to while away a few hours in Bloomsbury. They read newspapers or popular novels, or (like Virginia Woolf) read and wrote personal letters, which some could easily have done at home. Some merely slept for hours on end. Others turned up drunk, stole, hid, 'borrowed' or cut pages from books, cruised for sexual partners, or even started fights.

9

One user who was notorious for taking books out of the reading room was the Russian revolutionary Sergei Kravchinsky, known in London by the alias Sergius Stepniak. 'Stepniak' used to take books out of the room at lunchtime, but always returned them. He had done worse things: in 1878 he had assassinated Nikolai Mezentsov, the head of the Russian secret police. It was Kravchinsky's enthusiasm for books that killed him in the end: in December 1895 he was killed by a train at Chiswick, having wandered onto the track while reading a book.

A sexual liaison that began in the reading room involved Karl Marx's precocious London-born youngest daughter Eleanor (1855-1898), known in the family as 'Tussy'. Eleanor had the misfortune to fall in with the reptilian Edward Aveling in the reading room; a man who set out his views on the place as a pickup joint in an article published in the journal *Progress* in 1883. With his forked tongue coiled into his cheek, Aveling suggested in his article *Some Humours of the Reading Room at the British Museum* that 'a special district' under the dome should be 'set aside for ugly readers'. These, he said, should be kept out of the 'district' reserved for the 'well-favoured' by a special force of 'police, or, perhaps, retired prize-fighters, in some chaste uniform'.

Marx's daughter met Aveling in the reading room in 1883, the same year he had written his article about the place, which he also suggested might appear to visitors like 'so many animals imprisoned under a cavernous dome and girt round by books'. Aveling asked Eleanor to write a short biography of her father for *Progress*.

Eleanor and Edward became lovers, but Aveling convinced his new mistress that they could not marry because he was already married to somebody else (he was not). Furthermore, he persuaded her to claim that she was married to him, Aveling, to give their liaison an air of respectability. She therefore went about calling herself 'Mrs Aveling'. The fake marriage was a tactic used on several women by the Victorian murderer George Chapman, believed by some to be a likely suspect in the Jack the Ripper case. Chapman would take his mistresses away for a short holiday, then return and tell everybody that they had married.

Despite his dishonest nature, Edward Aveling became a significant member of the Marx circle in London, wrote on political issues and even translated some of Marx's writings. Eleanor's father is known to have been an enthusiast for phrenology, the now discredited pseudo-science that was supposed to allow the adept to discern the personalities of individuals by feeling the bumps on their skulls. New acquaintances would be checked for malign bumps by the great man himself, and sometimes by his friend the more expert Karl Pfaender, a German portrait-painter. Evidently neither of them found anything amiss with Aveling's skull.

Although there was never any genuine scientific basis for phrenology, the pseudo-science could still be weaponised and abused. In a disgraceful 1862 letter to Engels about the German social democrat Ferdinand Lassalle, Marx suggested that the shape of Lassalle's skull explained what Marx described as his 'peculiar' character.

While some were distracted from serious study in the reading room by hushed flirtations, others were perhaps too eccentric to be able to carry out a coherent programme of research, let alone write about their findings. In Virginia Woolf's 1922 novel *Jacob's Room*, the novelist introduces us to Miss Marchmont, a constant presence under the ornate papier mâché dome, who is working 'to confirm her philosophy that colour is sound – or, perhaps, it has something to do with music. She could never quite say, though it was not for lack of trying'.

David Lodge heads the chapters of his 1965 novel with quotations about the reading room from past users. At the start of Chapter IV we learn that Thomas Carlyle believed that:

there are several persons in a state of imbecility who come to read in the British Museum. I have been informed that there are several in that state who are sent there by their friends to pass away their time.

Another user, the poet W.B. Yeats, who was compiling a book of Irish fairy-stories, was evidently suffering from physical rather than mental problems:

I spent my days at the British Museum, and must, I think, have been very delicate, for I remember often putting off hour after hour consulting some necessary book because I shrank from lifting the heavy volumes of the catalogue.

Writing in 1860, the novelist William Makepeace Thackeray sang the room's praises:

It seems to me one cannot sit down in that place without a heart full of grateful reverence. I own to have said my grace at the table, and to have thanked Heaven for this my English birthright, freely to partake of these bountiful books and speak the truth I find there.

Some would say that Karl Marx, sitting at his desk in the old British Museum reading room, was out to challenge anything that resembled Thackeray's pious patriotism, and to find a new 'truth' unsuspected or perhaps ignored by many of his fellow-readers, under the paper dome.

When the reading room first opened in 1857, thousands of visitors came to admire its lofty false ceiling and other features. Sir Frederic Madden, then Keeper of Manuscripts at the BM, agreed that the Room was 'splendid' but confided to his diary that he thought it 'perfectly unsuited . . . to its purpose, and an example of reckless extravagance (having cost £150,000) occasioned by the undue influence of a foreigner'. One hundred and fifty thousand pounds in 1857 would be worth over nine million today.

The 'foreigner' mentioned by Madden was Antonio Panizzi (1797-1879) the *de facto* head of the BM from 1856 to 1866, who masterminded the construction of the reading room in the once-empty square courtyard of the museum. Panizzi was a political exile like Karl Marx: he had been forced to flee his native Italy in 1822.

Although the new reading room was supposed to resemble older domed spaces such as the Pantheon in Rome, originally a pagan temple, it was a state-of-the-art building for its time, constructed around a modern iron ribcage and with innovative solutions to the problems of ventilation and temperature control. It was also built at an impressive speed – just three years from first spade in the earth to the informal opening breakfast, with champagne and ices, on the second of May 1857.

The reading room under construction (Wellcome collection)

Photographs of the half-finished building show workmen in flat caps (and one in a top hat) using spades, pickaxes and very long wooden ladders, some of the men standing on the high iron with the nonchalant air of people loitering on a village green. An engraving of the construction shows draught horses being led away, having just delivered a load of iron on a long cart.

Although it had some hi-tech features when it first opened, the reading room did not have artificial light: this would have had to have been done via candles, gas-lights or oil-lamps in those days, and these would have posed a fire risk. Until electric lights could be installed, readers had to make do with whatever sunlight got through the smogs and grey clouds of London. Because of the fire risk, smoking was also banned in the reading room. Karl Marx, who was notorious for smoking far too many cheap cigars, would step outside to smoke in the museum's colonnade. Colonnade-smoking and pea-souper smogs also feature in David Lodge's British Museum novel.

When he could afford to, Marx took his lunch at the Museum Tavern in Great Russell Street just opposite the BM. This particular London watering-hole would have been very new when Marx started to visit: it still retains many of its Victorian features, and sells classic English pub food, including fish and chips, scotch egg, sausage and mash, and steak and ale pie.

The reading room's status as the beating heart of what was once called the British Museum Library was bound to be threatened by the expansion of its collection and the relocation of what is now called the British Library to its new premises at St Pancras. This was completed in 1997, the year Max Beerbohm's hero Enoch Soames was supposed to materialise in the reading room, having been thrown forward a century. For a short time, the reading room became a public reference library, the Walter and Leonore Annenberg Centre, but from 2007 to 2013 the space housed special exhibitions. This was achieved without moving the historic desks at which the likes of Charles Babbage, Samuel Beckett and Charles Darwin had once sat. A temporary floor was inserted above these.

One reason why the British Library had to move out of Bloomsbury was because its collection had, by the nineteen-nineties, grown way beyond the 'million books' mentioned by Thackeray. This was inevitable since the British Library is what is known as a 'copyright library': in theory a copy of every book published in the UK has to be sent to the BL. This had been the case before Panizzi, but the Italian was so insistent about enforcing this particular law that the library's holdings began to swell exponentially.

As the new millennium approached in the nineteen-nineties, the labyrinthine 'iron library' that had once filled the remaining courtyard of the British Museum was removed, and the area was covered with an ingenious glass ceiling. Since the year 2000 the old reading room, now faced in pure white stone, stands at the centre of an airy indoor courtyard, housing shops, seating and a café. The BM facades that face into what is now called the Great Court, which were unseen by the public for nearly a century and a half, are now the grand stone walls of a large room, visited by over a million people in 2021 alone.

At the time of writing (October 2022) the reading room Marx knew is closed to the public, and its future is uncertain.

Karl Marx not only used the old British Museum reading room himself: he also encouraged others to do so. In his 1886 memoir of the man he called 'Mohr', Marx's friend Wilhelm Liebknecht wrote:

About this time the magnificent reading room of the British Museum, with its inexhaustible treasures of books, had been built, and thither, where he passed a certain time every day, Marx drove us. To learn! To learn! This was the categorical imperative he frequently enough loudly shouted to us, but it also was expressed by his example, yea, by the sole aspect of this forever strenuously working mind.

While the rest of the fugitives were laying plans for the overthrow of the world and intoxicating themselves day by day, evening by evening with the hashish drink of: "Tomorrow it will start," we, the "sulphur-gang" the "bandits," the "scum of humanity," were sitting in the British Museum and trying to educate ourselves and to prepare arms and ammunition for the battles of the future.

Sometimes we would not have had a bite, but that would not prevent our going to the Museum. There were at least comfortable chairs to sit down on and in winter a cheering warmth, which were missing at home, if one had any "house" or "home" at all.

(Trans. Untermann, 1900)

The 'fugitives' Liebknecht mentions were the political exiles from various parts of the world who then lived in London, some in very straitened circumstances. By no means all of these would have described themselves as socialists. Joseph Conrad's intense and darkly comic 1907 novel *The Secret Agent*, set in 1886, depicts the grim world in which some of these exiles lived, and the way they interacted with home-grown British radicals.

Conrad's central character, Adolf Verloc, is, in theory, a dangerous London anarchist, but he is actually a secret agent working for a foreign power. In this role, he is supposed to be an *agent provocateur*, charged with spurring genuine radicals into action, giving them, as the saying goes, 'enough rope to hang themselves'; but in fact he is so lazy that he has to be threatened with penury before he takes any action at all. Verloc lives in Soho, as did the Marxes for many years. The plot of the book revolves around a disastrous attempt by Verloc to arrange a bombing outrage which will stir the British authorities into action.

In the novel, which, unlike so many of Conrad's tales, has nothing to do with the sea or boats, the ideas of the 'ticket-of-leave' anarchist Michaelis are reminiscent of those of Marx, especially his notion that capitalism must inevitably collapse: we just have to be prepared for this eventuality. A 'ticket-of-leave' in this context was a certificate that allowed a prisoner freedom on certain conditions. A year after Conrad's *Secret Agent* appeared, G.K. Chesterton published his novel *The Man Who Was Thursday*, also set in Victorian times, which, like Robert Louis Stevenson's 1885 story *The Dynamiter*, covers some of the same ground as Conrad's book.

*The Secret Agent* is very good on the dirty drabness of Victorian London. A well-connected Assistant Commissioner of police, doing a little bit of detective work on his own initiative, disguises himself as a man of more humble means and steps out alone:

His descent into the street was like the descent into a slimy aquarium from which the water had been run off. A murky, gloomy dampness enveloped him. The walls of the houses were wet, the mud of the roadway glistened with an effect of phosphorescence, and when he emerged into the Strand out of a narrow street by the side of Charing

Cross Station the genius of the locality assimilated him. He might have been but one more of the queer foreign fish that can be seen of an evening about there flitting round the dark corners.

The emotional keynote of Conrad's novel is resentment. Everybody resents the lives they are forced to live, the people they are forced to mix with and the way they have to make a living. An amoral bomb-maker nick-named the Professor clearly thinks of himself as a genius of European importance, yet lives as a lodger in in a cheap room in a house 'lost in a wilderness of poor houses':

His struggles, his privations, his hard work to raise himself in the social scale, had filled him with such an exalted conviction of his merits that it was extremely difficult for the world to treat him with justice . . .

In London, both Marx and Engels encountered secret agents and *agents provocateurs*, and were not always able to identify them as such. In June 1850 the two Germans, together with their friend August Willich, managed to get a letter published in the *Spectator*, in which they complained not only that their footsteps were dogged by British police spies 'who take down their notes very coolly every time any one enters the house or leaves it' but that they were also troubled by Prussian *agents provocateurs*, with their 'ferocious spouting' and 'rabid proposals'. These men would have been employed by the Prussian Minister of the Interior, who was none other than Marx's brother-in-law Ferdinand von Westphalen.

The aim of Ferdinand's agents was, as Marx, Engels and Willich explained in their *Spectator* letter, to gather evidence intended to persuade the British authorities to expel German radicals from London. The letter expresses the authors' opinion that the British police spies that they have spotted are 'anything but clean and respectable', that they are 'miserable' and also 'male prostitutes of the lowest order', and that their mere existence poses a threat to the British reputation for fairness and freedom. The authors also express their hope that there is not any kind of *entente cordiale* between the British and Prussian agents.

The 'arms and ammunition' Marx himself was preparing, both in and out of the British Museum, as Liebknecht hinted, 'for the battles of the future' comprised, among other things, his vast book *Capital*, which was left unfinished at his death in 1883. Marx only lived to see the first of the four volumes of *Capital* published, in German in 1867. A Russian translation was published in Marx's lifetime, but the first English translation, in which the slimy Edward Aveling had a hand, did not appear until 1887.

The current Penguin paperback translation is a wrist-snapping one thousand one hundred and fifty-two pages, or roughly four times the length of the average novel, which makes *Capital* another of those terribly important books that very few people have actually read. After Marx's death, volumes two and three were assembled from Marx's notes by his friend Frederick (or Friedrich) Engels. Volume four was edited by the philosopher Karl Kautsky.

The subtitle of *Capital* translates as *A Critique of Political Economy*. To put it very simply, the book was Marx's attempt to show that capitalism, at least as it was practised in the author's own day, was not a viable system for running the world's economy long-term, and that the various contradictions at the heart of the system were bound to cause it to collapse. Marx predicted that when this happened the workers themselves would take over, ushering in 'the dictatorship of the proletariat'.

Liebknecht repeatedly states in his memoir of Marx that *Capital* and the other work that his friend tackled in London could not have been done anywhere else. Britain was the most advanced industrial nation of the time, and perhaps the most committed to the capitalist system. Much of the technology on show here in the nineteenth century, some in the BM reading room itself, would have seemed futuristic to many foreign visitors. It was here, then, leaning over the railing at the very front of the capitalist ship, that Marx could draw conclusions about where exactly the vessel was heading.

When he first started to use the reading room, Marx immersed himself in back copies of *The Economist*, a weekly newspaper that was then only a few years old. The paper is still published, though now in the form of a magazine, and has a circulation of well over a million, if one includes the uptake of its electronic edition. Originally founded to speak up against the Corn Laws, Marx regarded it as the mouthpiece of that part of the bourgeoisie whom he described as 'the aristocracy of finance'. Later, Lenin called *The Economist* 'the journal that speaks for British millionaires'. In an edition chosen at random from 1849, there is a lot of detail about the cotton trade in various parts of the world, fears of a war with Russia, welcome news of declining deaths from cholera in London, and a story about an exploding sewer, also in the English capital.

In the prospectus published in advance of the first edition of *The Economist* in 1843, the editors promised 'an article on the elementary principles of political economy, applied to practical experience, covering the laws related to prices, wages, rent, exchange, revenue and taxes'. The hybrid field of political economy was of great importance for Marx's project: he published his *Contribution to the Critique of Political Economy*, a precursor to *Capital*, in 1859.

To write *Capital* well – to make it a sustained, significant, scientific contribution to the debate about capitalism, Marx not only needed to be in the world capital of capitalism itself – he also needed to be in the British Museum reading room, with its unique access to the vast range of disparate source materials that he could draw on to write his book, including old copies of *The Economist*.

Although Liebknecht did not always agree with Marx, and found fault with aspects of his approach (which makes him a good source on the man) Marx's friend was convinced that the work Marx was doing in the BM reading room and beyond was decidedly scientific: Liebknecht evoked the hallowed name of Charles Darwin no less than eight times in his short memoir of Marx. He claimed that:

Marx was one of the first to comprehend the importance of Darwin's investigations. Even before 1859, the year of the publication of the *Origin of Species* (by a singular coincidence also the year of the publication of Marx's *Critique of Political Economy*) Marx had recognised the epochal importance of Darwin, who, far from the noise and stir of the great cities, in his peaceful country home, was preparing a revolution similar to the one Marx was initiating himself at the turbulent centre of the world, only that he inserted his lever at a different place.

In the same way that Darwin studied his Galapagos finches and tried to discern the natural mechanism through which they had arrived at their particular forms, Marx was examining the various forms of capitalism, trying to work out how it would collapse, and how the proletariat it had created would emerge victorious from the rubble. Liebknecht seems not to have known that, though he did a great deal of work at his 'peaceful country home', Down House in Kent, Darwin had also conducted research at the British Museum.

Marx was able to take full advantage of the sources that he now had ready to hand in London because of his command of languages, his intelligence, his prodigious memory and his capacity for prolonged bouts of study and writing. Reading and taking notes in the reading room all day, he would sometimes return home and write all night. Here his insomnia also helped but, as we shall see, this way of life was no more sustainable than Marx thought capitalism itself was.

A busy day in the reading room in 1874 (Wellcome)

# Where All Road Lead

Though Liebknecht insisted that *Capital* could have been researched and written only in London, the book has a relevance way beyond Britain, which is hardly surprising given the background and early life of the author.

Karl Heinrich Marx was born in the ancient German city of Trier on the fifth of May 1818. Through both of his parents, he was descended from a distinguished line of rabbis, who had lived in Poland, Italy, the Netherlands and Hungary. Marx was also related to the Dutch Philips family, who founded the Philips electrical brand.

Marx's native town of Trier is very close to France, and in fact it had been under French control until 1815, when it was taken over by Prussia in the aftermath of the Napoleonic wars. In those days Germany was made up of many separate states, dominated by Prussia. The hide-bound, reactionary nature of many of these states meant that Germany was far behind Britain in modernisation and industrialisation. One consequence of this was that there was a German diaspora of economic and political refugees, seeking work in various places all over the world, including the Americas and Britain. Some of these dispersed Germans clubbed together into a political organisation called the Communist League, with whom Marx became deeply involved in the 1840s.

One consequence for the Marxes of the Prussian takeover of Trier was that, as Jews, they now suffered disadvantages under

Prussian law. In March 1812 a law had been passed that was very advantageous to the Prussian Jews, opening many professions to them, and giving them full citizenship. This law was, however, set aside by the Prussian king, Frederick William III (to whom Beethoven had dedicated his ninth symphony in 1824). His majesty reneged on a promise that Jews who had fought in his army would be allowed to work for the state, and between 1818 and 1819 excluded them from academic and state positions. The poet Heinrich Heine converted from Judaism to Christianity because as a Jew he would not have been allowed to take up an academic post. In the end, he never got into academia anyway.

Like Heine, Marx's father Heinrich converted to Christianity to minimise the disadvantages he would have suffered as a Jew under Prussian rule. This he did in 1816 or 1817. The rest of the family followed suit – the last to be baptised was Marx's mother Henriette, née Pressburg, who became a Christian in 1825, the same year as Heine. Like Heine, the Marxes converted to the Lutheran strand of Christianity, although Roman Catholicism was dominant in their part of Germany. This may have been an advantage for Karl when he came to live permanently in London. At the time, in the middle of the nineteenth century, many English people, who were predominantly Protestant, were very prejudiced against Catholics, although legislation had made it easier for followers of the old religion to prosper in English society.

Karl Marx attended the Friedrich-Wilhelm Gymnasium in Trier (in Germany the 'gymnasium' schools are intended to prepare the brighter pupils for higher education). At the University of Bonn, Marx made friends with the brother of his future wife, Jenny von Westphalen, to whom he became engaged at the age of eighteen (Jenny was four years older than Karl). As the 'von' part of her name suggests, Jenny, a noted beauty, was from an aristocratic family. She even had connections with the noble Wishart family of Scotland, and could claim the Scottish King James I as an ancestor (this was not the seventeenth-century King James I of England and IV of Scotland, but James I of Scotland, who died in 1437). Jenny's distinguished father Johann Ludwig von Westphalen befriended young Karl, shared some of his interests and served as something of a mentor.

Jenny Marx as a young woman

Mrs Marx's Scottish ancestry had some odd effects on the Marxes' lives later, when the family was living in London. Karl's attempt to pawn some of the family silver was delayed when the pawnbroker failed to understand how a down-at-heel German immigrant could lay his hands on pieces that looked like they belonged in some castle by a Scottish loch. As re-told by the socialist convert H.M. Hyndman, who had it from Jenny, Marx was unable to talk himself out of the *contretemps* with the pawn-broker because at the time his English was not very good. The man's suspicions were further aroused by the fact that Marx was evidently a Jew, and had come to his shop at night. He sent for the police, and the future author of *Capital* spent thirty-six hours detained at the station.

When Marx was reading through the works of Walter Scott with his daughter Eleanor, 'Tussy', as she was called, was distressed to find that some of her Scottish ancestors, as represented in Scott's historical novels, were no better than they should have been.

In 1836 Marx transferred from the university of Bonn to the university of Berlin, where he studied philosophy, indulged in prolonged bouts of overwork, annoyed his father by building up large debts, and seemed to show no interest in the question of how he was to earn a living when he eventually quitted the student life. In the event, he began to write for a new journal, the *Rheinische Zeitung*, of which he soon became editorial director. Although Marx's contributions to the journal were hardly radical, the Prussian censors closed down the *Rheinische Zeitung* in 1843.

Helene Demuth

Marx soon became joint editor of another new journal, the *Deutsche-Französische Jahrbücher*, to be published in Paris, where Karl and Jenny, who married in 1843, now set up house. Here they were joined by Helene Demuth, known as Lenchen, a servant of the von Westphalens who now became a servant of the Marxes. In 1844 Jenny Caroline, their first child, was born, and the Prussian government issued arrest warrants against the editors of the *Jahrbücher*, since they were supposed to have committed treason.

In the next year, Marx became a stateless refugee when he gave up his Prussian citizenship. He could not, however, escape the long arm of the Prussian authorities, who pressurised the French into expelling the Marxes from Paris. They moved to Brussels, where a second daughter, Jenny Laura, was born, and a son called Henry. All of the Marxes' daughters had the first name Jenny, after their mother. This is reminiscent of the daughters of

25

the Austrian empress Maria Theresa (1717-1780) who gave all her daughters the first name Maria, after herself. The most famous of these is Maria Antonia, known to history as Marie Antoinette.

By the time the Marx family reached the Belgian capital, Karl's thinking had moved very much to the left. Through intense study of the ideas of the German philosophers Hegel and Feuerbach, among others, and by reading the history of the French Revolution, Marx had come to the conclusion that the workers alone could bring about the changes humanity needed (Karl's Paris friend and distant relative the poet Heine had studied under Hegel himself in Berlin in the 1820s).

Through his work on the *Deutsche-Französische Jahrbücher* in Paris, Marx formed a friendship with the slightly younger fellow-Prussian Frederick Engels, whose name is always linked to that of Karl Marx, much as Lennon's is always linked to McCartney's, and Gilbert's to Sullivan's. A more evocative parallel is suggested in Isaiah Berlin's biography of Marx: the two men were like Moses and Aaron.

Another parallel was offered by Edgar Longuet, one of Marx's grandchildren. To him Engels and his grandfather were like Orestes and Pylades, buddies in the *Oresteia*, a trilogy of plays by Aeschylus, an ancient Greek writer whom Marx counted among his favourite authors, together with Shakespeare, Goethe and Diderot. Reading Shakespeare played a key role in the improvement of Marx's English, after he came to stay in England.

The exception that proved the rule of Marx and Engels' otherwise rich and enduring friendship was the rift that briefly opened between the two men in January 1863. When Engels' long-term mistress Mary Burns died in that month, Marx's letter of consolation to his old friend was barely sympathetic, and filled with his own petty concerns. Engels replied in suitably chilly style, but the two men could not remain estranged for long.

In 1844 Engels had submitted an article called *Outlines of a critique of national economy* to the *Jahrbücher,* which inspired Marx to read up on economics. Engels' article had been informed by his experience of how the national economy of Britain worked. He had gained this experience by working in the offices of his father's factory in Salford, Manchester: in fact he wrote his *Outline* while he was living there.

Marx visited London and Manchester with Engels in the summer of 1845. He returned to the English capital in the winter of 1847 to attend an important congress of the Communist League in Soho. The League asked Marx and Engels to draw up a manifesto: this became the famous *Communist Manifesto*, published in 1848, a year that saw revolutions in, among other places, France, Germany, the Netherlands, Hungary, Italy and Denmark. Readers should not get the impression that Marx and Engels' *Manifesto* caused these revolutions, or had much to do with them at all: the initial publication of this groundbreaking little book had almost no impact.

One impact that the 1848 revolutions had on Marx, the co-author of the *Communist Manifesto*, was that he was expelled from Brussels. He was now able to return to post-revolutionary Paris, at the invitation of the new republican government. A few weeks later he moved again, this time to post-revolutionary Cologne, where he and Engels founded a daily paper called the *Neue Rheinische Zeitung: Organ der Democratie.*

The revolutions of 1848 met with resistance from the reactionary authorities, and in May 1849 Marx was expelled from Cologne. The family returned to Paris, where they were, however, no longer welcome. Marx was told that he could remain in France only if he took up residence in southern Brittany, far from the capital, where the authorities assumed that he would be able to exert very little influence. Keen to revive the *Neue Rheinische Zeitung*, Marx returned to London at the end of August, 1849. From then on, he never lived anywhere else: he died in London in 1883, having spent roughly half his life in the English capital. One reason why London could serve as a safe haven for the Marxes was because there had been no revolution in England in 1848, and so there was no extreme reaction that meant that radicals might be victimised.

Marx's bitterness at the collapse of the 1848 revolution in France is expressed in his little book *The Eighteenth Brumaire of*

*Louis Bonaparte.* Brumaire ('misty') was one of the new months introduced after the French revolution of 1789. 'Louis Bonaparte' was the suave, broad-shouldered, philandering, chain-smoking Charles Louis Napoléon Bonaparte. After years of exile, during which he lived in much better style than the impoverished Marxes, this nephew of Napoleon Bonaparte returned to Paris to take up a seat in the National Assembly of the new Second Republic, in September 1848.

Partly because of widespread nostalgia for the days of the emperor Napoleon, his nephew was elected president of the new republic in December 1848. Threatened with having to stand down at the end of his first term, Louis staged a successful coup in December 1851, and declared himself emperor in 1852. He is now remembered as Emperor Napoleon III. Writing about the 1851 coup in his *Eighteenth Brumaire,* Marx wondered 'how a nation of thirty-six millions can be surprised by three swindlers, and taken to prison without resistance'. The 'three swindlers' were perhaps Louis, his half-brother Morny and the then minister of war, Jacques Leroy de Saint Arnaud.

Marx was quite clear that Louis' coup stank to high heaven: one consequence of it was that Karl's family (like the French king the 1848 revolution had removed) now had to move to London, a city that quite literally stank. The Great Stink of the summer of 1858 was caused by a deadly combination of unspeakable filth and hot weather. It was the unbearable stench of that year that persuaded the government to invest in the vast new sewage system proposed by the engineer Joseph Bazalgette. When Marx arrived in 1849 the London sewage system, such as it was, was already completely overwhelmed by the sheer volume of human, animal and industrial waste that was the inevitable product of a city of some three and a half million people, or around sixteen percent of the population of England, crowded into an area that corresponded roughly to a circle some fifteen miles wide.

The presence of industrial premises, belching smoke into the air and spewing noxious chemicals into the Thames, was a feature of London life that has no real equivalent today. People who could afford to heat their premises were using coal or wood, which only added to the poisonous atmosphere. Liebknecht commented that in a typical London garden, such as the one attached to one of Marx's homes, the grass and any paving were always the same colour – black. Buildings such as the British Museum would also be caked in a slimy black layer of soot, which was concentrated in any areas where the rain could not wash it off. This seemed to darken the shadows visible on the facades of buildings. Today most of London's older buildings look much better than they did a few decades ago, because of modern sand-blasting and deep-cleaning.

In London, the Marxes and their friends attempted to get at least some of the smoke out of their lungs by making regular visits to the wild expanse of Hampstead Heath. These walks happened on Sundays, when the entire family and accompanying friends would walk for an hour and a quarter from their poky home in Dean Street, with Lenchen, the family servant, carrying a picnic basket over her arm. After an *al fresco* lunch, the adult members of the expedition would either sleep or read newspapers, then discuss their contents, while the children ran around.

One imagines that Marx and his more political friends read newspapers differently from most people. Marx himself was a journalist, among other things, and in his journalism and his other writings he constantly referred to current events and topical issues. Himself and people he knew were liable to be mentioned in newspapers, and he often took issue with how other journalists covered important events.

Up on Hamstead Heath, donkeys would be ridden (as they still are in British seaside resorts) and during the walk home there would be singing, discussions about art and literature, and passages from Goethe's *Faust* recited from memory by Marx himself.

Back down in the smoke and dirt, within the fifteen-mile wide circle centred on Charing Cross, thousands were crammed into crumbling, obsolete housing with no modern amenities at all. Cross-infection between the obsolete sewage system and the drinking-water supply led to deadly cholera epidemics. An outbreak in 1848-9 killed over fifty thousand people. As the British learned again during the Covid pandemic that began in 2019, a concentration of infectious disease in one section of the population endangers everybody. Typhoid, which like cholera is spread by human waste, was a frequent visitor to London homes, and is thought by some to have killed Queen Victoria's husband, Prince Albert, in 1861.

According to *The Condition of the Working Class in England*, written by Marx's friend Frederick Engels and published in 1845, the 'rookeries' or slums of London did not only breed disease. Engels recognised that the grim lives many were forced to live in these places led to drunkenness and crime, making 'the British nation the most criminal in the world'. Many women turned to, or were forced into, prostitution, some at a shockingly young age: Engels mentions 'the 40,000 prostitutes who fill the streets of London every evening', who 'live upon the virtuous bourgeoisie'. Harsh treatment at the hands of the authorities and their employers tended to brutalise the proletariat, causing them to abandon hope, morality, self-respect and the ties of family and friendship.

*The Condition of the Working Class* draws on official statistics, government reports and the columns of reputable newspapers. Engels tells us that conditions such as those to be found in London could also be seen in other great industrialised British cities, such as Sheffield, Edinburgh and Manchester. Since he worked there in the family firm, Engels knew Manchester well. His guide to the poorer parts was his working-class mistress, the Irishwoman Mary Burns.

Engels describes London as a 'whirlpool', always ready to drag down the unwary. The American writer Jack London went further in his 1903 book *People of the Abyss*, about life in the Whitechapel area of the East End of London. Both Engels and Jack London noted how some misfortune, such as a period of illness, an injury at work, the death or desertion of a family member, a theft, the birth of an unwanted child, a petty crime, an ill-advised sexual encounter or just a random sacking could doom whole families to be sucked into the abyss of poverty, from which they found it very hard to extricate themselves.

As Engels observed in Manchester, injuries at work were all too common, and for many there was no safety-net to support them when they could no longer earn money to live. In many cases, injuries just added to the physical problems which the workers suffered because of poor health and life-long malnutrition:

In the throstle-room of the cotton mill at Manchester, in which I was employed, I do not remember to have seen one single tall, well-built girl; they were all short, dumpy, and badly-formed, decidedly ugly in the whole development of the figure. But apart from all these diseases and malformations, the limbs of the operatives suffer in still another way. The work between the machinery gives rise to multitudes of accidents of more or less serious nature, which have for the operative the secondary effect of unfitting him for his work more or less completely. The most common accident is the squeezing off of a single joint of a finger, somewhat less common the loss of the whole finger, half or a whole hand, an arm, etc., in the machinery. Lockjaw very often follows, even upon the lesser among these injuries, and brings death with it. Besides the deformed persons, a great number of maimed ones may be seen going about in Manchester; this one has lost an arm or a part of one, that one a foot, the third half a leg; it is like living in the midst of an army just returned from a campaign.

It is hard to believe some of the true stories related by Engels and Jack London in their writings about London. There were cases of people discovered, dead of starvation, in corners of their overcrowded, insanitary, fire-trap lodgings. Some families could not afford to bury their dead, and had to live alongside the corpses of family members. Marx reported such a death in all its ghastly detail in one of his articles about the English scene sent to a New York newspaper in 1853. This was the case of Ann Sandry, forty-three years old, who lived and died in Coal Lane, Shadwell, in London. 'The deceased was lying on a small heap of straw, without the slightest covering . . . five young children were sitting on the bare floor, crying from hunger and cold by the side of the mother's dead body'.

In the year before the death of Ann Sandry, Marx's own daughter Franzisca had died after a little over a year of life. She had not starved, but succumbed to bronchitis, and her mother tells us in her fragmentary autobiography that she had to frantically ask around for money for a coffin. Meanwhile the tiny corpse lay alone in one room of the family's two-room lodging, while the rest of the family made their beds on the floor in the other room. At last a French immigrant friend gave Jenny two pounds: she reflected that, though she now had a coffin, Franzisca had not even had a cradle to lie in when she was born.

To some extent, the conditions suffered by poor Londoners were relieved by parish provision or the work of charities, who provided soup-kitchens or places for the homeless to sleep. But like the sewage system before Bazalgette's innovations, charitable provision was overwhelmed by the sheer numbers of the needy. 'Parish provision' often meant the workhouse: the deep shame felt by people who were forced to take advantage of this particularly cold form of charity sometimes never left them. Engels characterised such places as prisons for people who had committed the crime of becoming poor. Sometimes the needy were not even offered this relief, if for instance they had not been born or raised locally.

The dread of the workhouse was remembered well into modern times by, for instance, people of my grandmother's generation, born at the turn of the nineteenth and twentieth centuries. The taint of the workhouse was so strong that some even refused to set foot in hospitals built where workhouses had once stood. The workhouses, and the various charities set up for destitute Londoners, served to smooth the sharp corners of a desperate situation, and salve the consciences of the bourgeoisie and the upper classes, whose wealth, security and status depended on the existence of these impoverished workers.

The hypocritical Victorians were past masters at the art of victim-blaming, asserting that the poor had only themselves to thank, and that they brought poverty on themselves through their drunkenness, idleness, improvidence, wilful ignorance and general immorality. This attitude still survives in the pages of some of England's right-wing tabloid newspapers, where so-called 'benefits scroungers' are singled out for criticism and blamed for all the ills of society in general.

Engels was quite clear that poverty-stricken unemployed Londoners were simply workers who were not needed in recession times, who would be needed again in the boom times, when unemployment fell. Engels, Marx and others noted the boom and bust pattern of capitalist economies; something that is still with us today. From the point of view of the communists and socialists of the nineteenth century, this painful see-saw was a weakness of the capitalist system which indicated that it was not sustainable in the longer term. The ever-present 'whirlpool' or 'abyss' that threatened poor workers made them desperate to work, and, when they had work, to hang on to their jobs at all costs, however grinding or poorly-paid they were. Better to be worked to death than to starve to death in a state of what was seen as shameful idleness.

Despite their evident helplessness, Marx saw in the workers – the proletariat – the potential for a revolution that would overturn the capitalist system, de-throne the rich and privileged rulers of the world, and establish a much fairer system – the aforementioned 'dictatorship of the proletariat'. The German saw this as an inevitable stage of evolution, following on from the industrial revolution that had created the proletariat, in the form familiar to Marx, in the first place.

In his *Condition of the Working Class in England*, Frederick Engels mentioned features of London life that will be familiar to modern Londoners. People paid high prices to live in overcrowded, sub-standard accommodation, there was a great deal of rough-sleeping and street-begging, and the capital seemed to be a city of strangers: thousands surged up and down the streets without acknowledging each other, as they might in smaller settlements, where, even today, strangers might be greeted in the street with a 'hello'.

Engels also noted the constant change in London: the look and character of whole sections of the great city could change, seemingly overnight, so that the area would hardly be recognisable to an old resident re-visiting after just a couple of years. Returning in 1878, after an absence of fifteen years, Liebknecht wrote:

I rubbed my eyes; was this the city in which I had lived for nearly half a generation and of which I then knew every street, every corner? Some things were still as of old, but how much was new and strange! And even the familiar objects changed by the strange surroundings. Streets gone, sections disappeared, new streets, new buildings and the general aspect so changed that in a place where I formerly could have found my way blindfolded I had to take refuge in a cab in order to get to my near goal.

One solution to the problem of the slums, which probably felt as if it was in step with the ever-changing nature of the city, was to demolish whole communities to make way for new roads or railways. This did not, however, solve anything: the slum people just moved elsewhere, as we shall see.

Engels quotes from contemporary reports which noticed how, in London, scenes of crushing poverty existed alongside extraordinary wealth. He found this in *The Times*:

It is indeed a monstrous state of things! Enjoyment the most absolute, that bodily ease, intellectual excitement, or the more innocent pleasures of sense can supply to man's craving, brought in close contact with the most unmitigated misery! Wealth, from its bright saloons, laughing – an insolently heedless laugh – at the unknown wounds of want!

The *Times* writer's image of rich people in 'bright saloons' laughing at the needy is powerful, but in fact many of the wealthiest Londoners were only in the city during the correct social season, from April to August. This meant that their fine London houses were mothballed for seven or more months out of the year, while they stayed at their suburban villas or country seats, or took capacious lodgings at Bath, or wintered in the south of France, or in Italy.

When in London, many 'gentlemen' spent much of their time at their club: a male-only environment where they could eat, drink, read newspapers, use the (often excellent) club library, and even stay overnight. While thousands slept in the streets or (illegally) in the London parks, Buckingham Palace, with its hundreds of rooms, stood practically empty most of the time, as Queen Victoria was seldom there.

Engels in 1872

While workers lucky enough to find employment worked long, weary hours for very little pay, some members of the aristocracy and the upper middle class hardly had to lift a finger: everything was done for them by servants. They didn't even have to venture out to buy new clothes: the most fashionable tailors and dress-makers would come to them. For active spirits like Florence Nightingale the leisured life was wearying in itself: in her book *Cassandra* (1852) she compared idle married women to 'those we may not name' (meaning prostitutes) and complained that, though they might be involved in charitable schemes such as 'schooling for the poor' they only spent 'an idle half hour' on such things 'between luncheon and driving out in the carriage'.

Twenty-first century readers will have got a lot of their ideas about conditions in Victorian times from the more socially-aware novels of the period, which are still in print and are frequently turned into feature films or TV series. Marx the widely-read theorist had had has hands on exactly the same books. In an 1855 article for a German paper called the *Neue Oder-Zeitung* he wrote about how 'the present splendid brotherhood of fiction-writers in England', including Dickens, Thackeray and Mrs Gaskell had shown the English middle class to be 'full of presumption, affectation, petty tyranny and ignorance'.

Marx died too early to have read George and Weedon Grossmith's novel *The Diary of a Nobody*, which was first published in book form in 1892. This comic classic pokes affectionate fun at Charles Pooter, a London clerk who lives with his family at their home 'The Laurels' in Holloway. Pooter is no tyrant, petty or otherwise; and is in fact bewildered by the lack of control he has over his family, or events.

Pooter has an almost crushing respect for people in the class above him – represented in the novel by his boss Mr Perkupp. He is also desperate to join Perkupp's class, or at least to be regarded as a member of it, worthy of the respect that he is continually, frustratingly, denied. Like a typical bourgeois, Pooter is also obsessed with his house and the possessions it contains – possessions which he hopes will create the impression that he is a truly impressive person – not a 'nobody' at all. And he is desperate that his wayward son Lupin should continue the family's upward trajectory, and not reverse it through laziness and generally irresponsible behaviour.

Although Charles Dickens in particular wrote some powerful evocations of Victorian London, many people get their ideas about this time and place from the Sherlock Holmes stories of Arthur Conan Doyle, or screen adaptations thereof. The first Holmes story did not appear until after Marx's death, but the elements of the Holmes milieu were in place by the time the German arrived in London in 1849. Smoke and fog had been part of London life for centuries, as had cobbled streets; and gas street-lighting had been in use for decades (in fact London still has some gas street-lights). The iconic hansom cab had been patented by the Yorkshireman Joseph Hansom in 1834, and the unmistakable Palace of Westminster, also known as the Houses of Parliament, were under construction when Marx arrived in the English capital.

By 1849 Queen Victoria, born the year after Karl Marx, had reached the age of thirty, and had been reigning for a dozen years. She had been married to her beloved Albert for nine years, and had borne nine children, including her second child and first son Albert, known as Bertie, who would succeed her as King Edward VII in 1901. On one level, Prince Albert was just another member of the nineteenth-century German diaspora, like Marx and many of his friends and associates. Victoria herself was a representative of the House of Hanover, claiming the throne via King George I, the closest living Protestant relative of Queen Anne, who became King of England on this basis, despite the fact that he was a foreign prince.

In the year Marx came to London to stay, Victoria was on her third Prime Minister, the bewhiskered Whig Lord John Russell, who was then enjoying the first of his two periods in Downing Street. Though he was the son of a duke, as a Whig Russell was supposed to be on the side of what Marx called the bourgeoisie, and working to take power out of the hands of the landed aristocracy. But in Marx's opinion, made very clear in a series of articles on the noble lord published in the *Neue Oder-Zeitung* in 1855, Russell adjusted his own opinions and convictions whenever such an adjustment seemed likely to get him into, or keep him in, a coveted post such as that of Prime Minister. To Marx, this made him what we would now call a 'lightweight':

The whole man is one false pretence, his whole life a lie, all his activity a continuous chain of petty intrigues for the achievement of shabby ends – the devouring of public money and the usurpation of the mere semblance of power . . . Placed by birth, connections, and social accidents on a colossal pedestal, he always remained the same homunculus – a dwarf dancing on the tip of a pyramid. History has, perhaps, never exhibited any other man – so great in pettiness.

(From the *Neue Oder-Zeitung*, No. 377, August 15, 1855)

Here Marx may be contradicting himself – his picture of Lord John Russell is remarkably similar to his view of Napoleon III in his *Eighteenth Brumaire* (1852). Like his response to the third Napoleon, Marx's articles on Russell show the German's talent for mockery, his grasp of detail, his excellent political memory, and his knowledge of literature, including Shakespeare, Greek mythology and Jonathan Swift's *Gulliver's Travels*.

Marx wrote in a similar vein about the future Prime Minister Lord Palmerston in an article published in an American newspaper in 1853, when Palmerston was still Home Secretary. For Marx, his lordship succeeded because of his 'most minute knowledge of Parliamentary tricks, parties, and men . . . secured from any surprise by his cynic impudence'. As we shall see, Marx was also quite prepared to entertain the possibility that Palmerston was a traitor, in league with and in the pay of Russia.

The author of *Capital* certainly knew, or thought he knew, about Palmerston: strange to say, Palmerston himself had an opportunity to learn about Marx, even when the latter was an impoverished immigrant living in cramped digs in Soho. When his lordship was Foreign Secretary, a report about the activities of Marx and his London comrades was sent to the Foreign Office from the Prussian Minister of the Interior, Baron Otto von Manteuffel.

The report suggested that, at least in the spring of 1850, 'one of the German Societies under Marx, Wolff, Engels, Seidel' which met upstairs at the Red Lion pub at number twenty, Great Windmill Street, Soho, was plotting to assassinate Queen Victoria, and indeed most of the crowned heads of Europe. The report stated that Marx and the others were confident that they had bloodthirsty minions scattered all over the continent, ready to hang or guillotine heads of state and others, including Queen Victoria's children. The report also recounted a story about Marx himself telling a young German called Linde that, because he had spoken against Marx and his circle, he had been condemned to death.

Robert Payne reproduces the Prussian report in full in his book *The Unknown Karl Marx*, and states that 'there is some reason to believe that the report . . . accurately reflects the intentions of the revolutionaries'. Other commentators are more sceptical: Francis Wheen writes that it is 'manifestly absurd', and the surviving evidence (or rather lack of it) suggests that the British government took no action, although similar concerns were also conveyed to the authorities by the Austrians.

The action of the Prussians and the Austrians in trying to persuade the British authorities to regard London's German-speaking political refugees as a threat is reminiscent of the efforts of the unnamed embassy in Conrad's novel *The Secret Agent*. Here the sinister First Secretary, Mr Vladimir, is irritated by the complacency of the British ruling class, 'the imbecile bourgeoisie' who 'make themselves the accomplices of the very people whose aim is to drive them out of their houses to starve in ditches'. 'What they want just now,' Vladimir adds, during a tense encounter with the book's hero, Verloc, 'is a jolly good scare'.

However 'manifestly absurd' the report sent to Palmerston may have been, it got one thing right: the Red Lion in Soho was an important meeting-place for Marx's associates in London. In this very place in 1847, the League asked Marx and Engels to write their *Communist Manifesto*. A shiny metal plaque at street level reminds passers-by of this fact, though the bar is now no longer called the Red Lion, but B@1. It still looks like a classic London watering-hole, however, and can be found on the corner of Great Windmill and Archer Streets.

As the Red Lion, the building was the London headquarters of the Communist League, and also of the German Workers' Educational Society. Marx was involved with both, and argued, lectured, planned, organised, ate, drank, smoked and played chess at the Red Lion. According to Engels' history of the Communist League, written in 1885, the Educational Society 'served the

League as a recruiting ground for new members'. One can imagine Marx, Engels and others looking out for intelligent, politically astute Society members, and taking them aside for a private little talk about communism.

Wilhelm Liebknecht

# The English Context

Britain had not undergone a revolution in 1848, that great year of revolutions, but that is not to say that the country was slumbering in a state of political contentment. Given the vast inequalities that were all too obvious, the pitiful condition of the least fortunate, and the way politicians like the Prime Minister Lord John Russell were able to skirt round the big issues and still remain in power, it is hardly surprising that many people in all walks of life were extremely discontented, and crying out for change.

Since 1838 the Chartists had been calling for reforms that went beyond the limited changes brought about after the Reform Act of 1832, reforms for which Russell was all too ready to claim the credit. Although the 1832 Act improved the system whereby MPs were elected to the House of Commons, after 1832 only about eighteen percent of adult males were eligible to vote, and no women. One rule that excluded many men from voting in elections was the property qualification, which disqualified anyone not owning property worth ten pounds or more (or over seven hundred pounds at today's values).

The Chartists wanted ordinary men to be able to vote: they also wanted ordinary people in general to be able to stay out of the dreaded workhouses of the time. The prospect of incarceration in one of these prisons for the poor was brought closer to many struggling people after the Poor Law Amendment Act of 1834, which meant that workhouses were no longer supposed to provide 'outdoor relief' to the needy. Outdoor relief was the nineteenth-century equivalent to modern state benefits paid to the unemployed, people in low-paid work, retired people or those whose disabilities or poor health makes it impossible for them to support themselves by working. Under the 1834 Act, those in distress would have to go straight into the workhouse, or go without.

In his book on Chartism, published in 1839, the Scottish thinker Thomas Carlyle tried to understand the mentality of the Poor Law Commissioners who wanted to incarcerate people whose income happened to drop below a certain level, and thus take their homes from them, break up their families and submit them to shame and humiliation. The Commissioners, Carlyle stated, were 'not tigers; they are filled with an idea of a theory' that the threat of the workhouse would force those previously eligible to receive outdoor relief to find work, thus, as Carlyle suggests with his tongue in his cheek, ushering in a new age of 'industry, frugality, fertility, rise of wages, peace on earth and goodwill towards men'.

The abolition of outdoor relief might be compared to some surreal plan whereby those in charge of the modern National Health Service in England decide that broken legs will no longer be treated for free. This will surely encourage people to stop breaking their legs, they tell themselves. But of course people will continue to break their legs from time to time, as inevitably as Carlyle, Marx, Engels and many others understood that some workers would fail to find work, while others would be quite unable to work.

Anger about the Poor Law Amendment Act fuelled Chartist attempts to broaden the electorate, in the hope that a parliament elected by ordinary people would not pass laws that made life so much harder for those workers who always felt the familiar whirlpool of future destitution sucking at them from below. In their People's Charter, the Chartists advocated almost universal adult male suffrage, wages for MPs, the abolition of the property qualification for MPs, voting by secret ballot, and an end to the system whereby some MPs represented a very small number of voters, while others represented far more. All of the Chartists' demands have been met in the modern British system, except for their idea that there should be a general election every year.

The annual elections idea was supposed to guard against corruption in politics, as was the Chartists' proposal for a secret ballot. If nobody could ever find out for sure how you had voted, then nobody could punish you for voting in a way they disapproved of, and the idea of bribing somebody to vote in a particular way would be pointless: he might take your bribe, vote the opposite way, then lie about how he had voted.

From his new vantage-point in London, Karl Marx was able to observe the shenanigans surrounding the British general election of 1852, and to report on them for a New York newspaper. Despite attempts to legislate against corruption in elections, 1852 saw shocking abuses, including widespread bribery and intimidation. Quoting, for the benefit of his American readers, from the *People's Paper*, a Chartist newspaper founded in the election year of 1852, Marx included copy on events in Limerick, where eight people had been killed by soldiers detailed to prevent anyone voting for the Whig or Liberal party (the whole of Ireland was then under British control, and returned MPs to Westminster). Among the less harmful abuses were the 'election entertainments' (as depicted by the artist William Hogarth in the previous century) where candidates paid for electors to get very drunk, in the hope that they might vote for the candidate who had stood them so many drinks.

In his account of the Chartist role in the 1852 elections, Marx included details of the odd tradition of the 'show of hands' that preceded the formal vote. At a typical hustings, the rival candidates would speak, then there would be a show of hands among the assembled men. The point was that the majority of the men who attended the hustings and showed their hands were usually not actually qualified to vote. Time and again, in 1852, the show of hands was in favour of a Chartist candidate, while the actual voters – the privileged eighteen percent of men – voted either Whig or Tory.

In some of his American articles about the 1852 election, Marx set out his own opinion of the various types of Whigs and

Tories – they belonged 'more or less to the past' while those agitating for Free Trade represented the increasingly powerful bourgeoisie, the 'Manchester School' of manufacturers who wanted to 'eradicate the last arrogant remains of feudal society', meaning the aristocracy. Marx asserted that the real enemies of the bourgeoisie were the Chartists: 'the carrying of their Universal Suffrage in England would . . . be a far more socialistic measure than anything that has been honoured with that name on the Continent'. It would lead to '*the political supremacy of the working class*' (Marx's italics).

Although some Chartists were ready for armed insurrection, the organisation was very much focused on the compilation of vast petitions which many had signed because they wanted to see the People's Charter become law. While revolutions swept across the Continent in 1848, on April the tenth of that year some twenty thousand Chartists, led by the charismatic MP Feargus O'Connor, held a mass meeting on Kennington Common in London.

The Royal Collection possesses two remarkable photographs of this protest, taken by William Edward Kilburn. They are remarkable in part because they were taken just a few years after the Frenchman Louis Daguerre invented this particular type of photography – the daguerrotype – and also because the pictures were bought by Prince Albert, Queen Victoria's husband.

Even in bright sunlight, the daguerrotype process required long exposures, so that many elements in the pictures of the Kennington Common gathering are blurred and smeared. The overall impression is of a dark mass of hundreds of men, and a few women, children, horses and horse-drawn vehicles covering the surface of the common, at the edge of which stands a fine house and a building with a tall industrial-looking chimney. Some of the women wear the fashionable plaid shawls of the time, and everyone is sporting a hat, cap or bonnet of some kind: the tall, dark, cylindrical top-hats that are often to be met with in early photographs taken in England are much in evidence.

The original idea of the Chartists gathered on the Common had been to march *en masse* to Parliament, to present their new petition. They were prevented by the thousands of soldiers, special constables and other volunteers who had been deployed to stop them. Among the volunteers, who were issued with truncheons and white arm-bands, were the future British prime minister W.E. Gladstone, and Louis Napoleon, later Emperor Napoleon III of France, who was characterised as a swindler in Marx's *Brumaire* book. What we might call 'operation stop the Chartists' was led by none other than the Duke of Wellington, who was then nearly eighty years old.

His plans frustrated by the forces ranged against him, Feargus O'Connor agreed that the great petition would be carried to Parliament in three cabs, and that the crowd at Kennington would disperse. Although Marx wrote approvingly about the role of the Chartists in the 1852 election, and even mentioned the revival of the Chartist cause, Engels saw the events of the tenth of April 1848 as the end of Chartism. In 1885 he wrote in the then new socialist newspaper the *Commonweal* that:

At the very moment when Chartism was bound to assert itself in its full strength [i.e., in 1848, the year of revolutions] it collapsed internally, before even it collapsed externally on the 10th of April, 1848. The action of the working-class was thrust into the background. The capitalist class triumphed along the whole line.

Parliament tried to complete the humiliation of the Chartists in 1848 by having the petition examined, and reporting that, rather than the nearly six million signatures O'Connor had boasted of in the House of Commons, there were actually rather fewer than two million genuine signatures, that some people had signed their names several times, and that some wags had signed themselves as Queen Victoria or the Duke of Wellington. There were also signatures that read 'Pugnose', 'Longnose', 'Flatnose' etc.

Of course Parliament in general had no interest in anyone taking any of the Chartist petitions seriously: the Members of the House of Commons had been elected by the privileged eighteen percent of men; if the remaining eighty-two percent could vote, the new voters might change the whole political landscape, help form a new party, and unseat large numbers of sitting MPs. The

Chartist demand that MPs themselves should be paid might mean that genuine working men might end up walking the hallowed halls of Westminster, destroying the Commons' reputation as the best gentlemen's club in London.

From around 1852 it became evident that the great Chartist leader Feargus O'Connor was becoming mentally unstable. His behaviour waxed erratic and even violent: some have attributed this change to syphilis. Although historians disagree about the health of the Chartist movement as a whole in the 1850s, in London after the middle of the nineteenth century Marx and Engels were witnessing both the slow decline of Chartism, and the merging of Chartism, and of individual Chartists, into the various radical groups that existed in England at the time, some of which were new and decidedly exotic imports.

Much of Marx's time in London was taken up either supporting, encouraging, leading and writing for and about such groups, or opposing groups or individuals with whom he found he could not agree. Sometimes Marx's bitter disagreements had to do with clashing personalities as well as conflicting ideologies. We are talking here about the time the great man did not spend studying in the British Museum reading room, writing at home, or interacting with family and friends.

One of the prominent Chartists whom Marx came to know well was Ernest Jones. Jones was only a year younger than Marx, and like Marx had been born in Germany, where his British father owned a farm. The family did not return to Britain until Ernest was nineteen years old. In England, Ernest seemed set to live the life of a wealthy lawyer, but financial problems made him susceptible to Chartist ideas.

Jones's political poems, published as *Chartist Songs*, became very popular, though the tone and subject-matter of Jones's verses are more to do with violent revolution than the peaceful delivery of petitions to Parliament in hansom cabs. In the poem *Onward* Jones groups together 'worn-out nobles, priests and kings'; in other poems he identifies bankers, including the officers of the Bank of England, as 'usurers'. In *A Song for the People* and elsewhere Jones celebrates what he sees as the inevitable end of the oppressors, who will be ground in the dust as surely as King Charles I was beheaded in 1649:

> In the days of old—when hearts beat bold,
> To the flap of Freedom's wing,
> The dust at our feet—was the winding sheet,
> That wrapt a headless king.

If nothing else, Jones's *Song for the People* is a reminder that the British were no strangers to revolution, despite the fact that they managed to avoid one in 1848. Not only did we behead a king in London in 1649 – the country was run as a republic until the Restoration of 1660. During this interregnum, many British groups including the Quakers, the Levellers, the Ranters and the Diggers experimented with new ways of living in communities: some of these involved equality for women and the sharing of property.

The Restoration of King Charles II was itself was a kind of revolution or coup, as was the so-called Glorious Revolution of 1688. This was when Charles's brother the Roman Catholic King James II was unseated, partly because of his religion. The explosion of commerce and innovation that put Britain in such a leading position in the world in Marx's day was another revolution – the Industrial Revolution – something that was bound up with the culture of the British non-conformists: religious dissenters such as the Unitarians, the Quakers and the Methodists.

The Chartists valued Ernest Jones not only as a poet and song-writer but also as a leader and a speaker – he spoke after O'Connor at Kennington on that fateful day in April 1848. Less than two months after he had spoken at Kennington, Jones was arrested in Manchester and charged with sedition and unlawful assembly. He was imprisoned for two years, emerged broken in health, and found his beloved Chartism in a similarly parlous state. From 1852 he published an important Chartist newspaper –

*The People's Paper*, which Marx read, cited and wrote for. The *Paper* was part of Jones's attempt to keep Chartism alive.

In his revealing *Memoir* of Marx, Wilhelm Liebknecht described Ernest Jones and his fellow-Chartist G.J. Harney, both of whom he met 'in Marx's house and company', as:

the leaders of the English working-class movement, the spartanic Julian Harney, the eloquent tribune and ardent journalist Ernest Jones, the last two great representatives of Chartism which grew into socialism . . .

Liebknecht had also encountered Robert Owen, the industrialist turned socialist, who, among others, had tried to support Ernest Jones through some lean times. As Liebknecht explained, Owen was:

the aged patriarch of socialism, by far the most comprehensive, penetrating and practical of all the predecessors of scientific socialism. We were at the gathering to celebrate his eightieth birthday and I had the good fortune to visit him frequently at his house . . .

Another of Marx's associates who came to know Ernest Jones in London was the radical German tailor Friedrich Lessner, who called him

the most popular and efficient leader of the Chartists, [who] occasionally visited our Society, where I had the opportunity to get to know that courageous and self-sacrificing agitator. Jones was small but well-knit . . . He could both write and speak German and he was one of the few Chartists who at the same time understood and preached socialism.

Lessner recalled how, on Kennington Common in '48, Jones had told the people:

not to fear the pitiful men of the law, the police, the soldiers or the shopkeepers sworn in as special constables who ran away from a couple of street urchins. "Down with the ministry! Dissolve Parliament! The Charter and no capitulation!"

The radical tailor claimed to have been there at Kennington on the day in question, together with some other members of the Communist League, a group Marx had a lot to do with after he settled in London. Lessner's friend Georg Eccarius was there as well, and was evidently ready for a fight: he came armed with 'a big pair of tailor's scissors, sharpened till they glistened, with which he intended to defend himself against the attacks of the constables'. Lessner was aware that one of these constables was the Frenchman who would later become Emperor Napoleon III: the German tailor refers to him as 'Napoleon the Little'.

Lessner was more impressed with Marx, whom he first met in London around 1848:

Marx was then still a young man, about 28 years old, but he greatly impressed us all. He was of medium height, broad-shouldered, powerful in build and energetic in his deportment. His brow was high and finely shaped, his hair thick and pitch-black, his gaze piercing. His mouth already had the sarcastic line that his opponents feared so much. Marx was a born leader of the people. His speech was brief, convincing and compelling in its logic. He never said a superfluous word; every sentence was a thought and every thought was a necessary link in the chain of his demonstration. Marx had nothing of the dreamer about him.

From *Reminiscences of Marx and Engels*, 1957

Lessner was less impressed by Engels, 'Marx's spiritual brother', whom he said looked 'more like a smart young lieutenant of the guard than a scholar'. This suggests that Lessner set great store by learning: not for him one modern attitude, pioneered by characters like former US president Donald Trump, that experts have no place in politics, and that learned advice should be ignored.

In his 1885 history of the Communist League, Engels remarked that German tailors (like Lessner) were 'the central force of the League' and that they seemed to be everywhere in the late 1840s and early 1850s; particularly in Switzerland, London and Paris. Engels claimed that in the French capital the Germans completely dominated the tailoring business, so that a Norwegian tailor he came to know there learned fluent German after eighteen months in the city, but remained almost completely ignorant of French.

Despite their devotion to the cause, in his history of the League Engels shares some reservations about tailors as revolutionaries. Like other skilled craftsmen, they tended to work alone or in small groups, and many aspired to run their own tailoring businesses, and thus become members of the petty bourgeoisie, or 'an appendage of the petty bourgeoisie'. They were not 'proper' proletarians in that they were not unskilled workers exploited in large numbers by big capitalists.

Engels' attitude to the tailors as revealed in his Communist League history is therefore a nice practical demonstration of some of his and Marx's ideas about future revolutions: they had to be led by the true proletariat to be valid and to have a chance of lasting success. Engels' treatment of the tailors in his Communist League history also shows how men like Marx and Engels had to take an interest in the details of different industries like tailoring. Since the Engels family business was to do with cotton, Marx's friend was bound to be rather well-informed about aspects of the rag trade.

For the numbers of proletarians to reach what we would now call a 'critical mass', making the 'right kind of revolution' inevitable, skilled workers like the tailors had to become de-skilled factory hands. Engels saw this happening in the tailoring business as the manufacture of ready-made or 'off the peg' clothes became more dominant. This was what he called 'the exploitation of tailoring on a large scale, what is now called the manufacture of ready-made clothes, by the conversion of handicraft tailoring into a domestic industry working for a big capitalist'.

Although Engels claimed that in the 1850s the ready-made clothing trade was not much developed, twenty years later it was conspicuously successful, and becoming dominant. The firm of E. Moses and Sons, founded by the son of a Jewish immigrant from Alsace, had splendid shops in London, Bradford and Sheffield that specialised in men's ready-made suits. There is good evidence that Karl Marx availed himself of their services in 1871, and bought a grey suit which he wore to a conference at the Hague in 1872. Journalists covering the conference remarked that in his new threads 'Dr Marx, the godfather of terrorism and chaos' looked like a gentleman farmer, or a well-to-do tourist.

We know rather more about the German Marxist tailor Friedrich Lessner than we do about the other German tailors whom Engels described as the backbone of the London radicals. According to his own recollections of Marx and the others, Lessner was converted to communism in Hamburg in 1846 and was at first a devotee of the teachings of the German radical Wilhelm Weitling (1808-1871) who was himself a tailor, among other things.

According to Marx, as quoted in Engels' *History of the Communist League*, Weitling's book *Guarantees of Harmony and Freedom* (1842) represented an important step forward for communism, but by the time Engels met Weitling in Brussels he seemed haunted and deluded, and members of the Communist League were beginning to find his brand of communism inadequate. Engels tells us that Mr and Mrs Marx entertained Weitling in Brussels 'with almost superhuman forbearance' because of his tendency to fall out with people.

For Lessner, reading and understanding Marx and Engels' *Communist Manifesto* set him on a path away from the 'enthusiasm and fancy' of Weitling and towards Marx's approach which, Lessner implied, was based more on scientific knowledge and less on a reliance on human good will.

That he was at times surrounded by tailors is reflected in the first chapter of Karl Marx's masterpiece, his book *Capital*, the first volume of which (the only one published during his lifetime) came out in German in 1867. Here, in a discussion of 'the dual character of labour embodied in commodities' he explains why a finished suit has more value than the length of cloth from which it was made: the value is added by human labour. Human labour is not, however, the only source of the value of the finished suit. It and the cloth from which it was made are ultimately derived from nature: the sunlight and water that cause the grass to grow, that feeds the wool-bearing sheep, etc.

The Chartist Ernest Jones

Liebknecht's description of the Chartist Ernest Jones as an 'eloquent tribune and ardent journalist' was probably meant to reference both his newspaper work and his poetry-writing. These were not mutually exclusive, as Chartist newspapers were noted for the amount of verse they published. Much of Marx's career up to the time he arrived in London had been concerned with trying to launch and sustain radical newspapers that were suppressed by the authorities, in Germany, France and Belgium.

It seems that, like Jones, the leaders of all the radical political movements of the time felt that some sort of newspaper was indispensable to their cause. This meant that many fiery radicals had to become journalists, editors, and publishers, able to keep track of costs and income, interact with printers, arrange for advertising, publicity and distribution, and stick to hard deadlines. With luck, the printed organ of the relevant group might turn a profit, but there were factors that militated against such an outcome.

Until 1855 the British authorities suppressed free speech via newspapers by making it very expensive to publish a newspaper of any political complexion. In a speech given at Rochdale in 1877, the Quaker politician John Bright remembered the effect of this legislation. It meant that the newspaper proprietors had to pay four pence to the government for every copy they printed: this paid for the official stamp that every copy had to bear. The proprietors also had to pay a tax on every advertisement they carried.

The result was that newspapers tended to cost around seven pence retail, equivalent in 1850 to about three pounds today. By 1877, Bright pointed out, the same newspapers might cost just a penny or even half a penny. The prohibitive cost of publishing newspapers under the old Stamp Act meant that they were beyond the pockets of ordinary working people, so that any radical workers' paper was bound to have an uncertain future. Jones's *People's Paper* folded after just six years, and the founder's own finances were uncertain until he resumed his legal practice around 1859.

Jones was lucky to have his legal training and qualifications to fall back on: Karl Marx, whom Jones had come to know through the aforementioned G.J. Harney, had no such bankable skills. In this respect Marx was worse off than the many poor German workers who came to London at this time: at least they could turn their hand to factory work, labouring, or aspects of the building trade, or use craft skills they had acquired at home. Ernest Jones features in Jenny Marx's fragmentary autobiography, *Short Sketch of an Eventful Life*. Here Marx's long-suffering wife tells us that Jones 'paid us long and frequent visits' around 1852, when the Marxes were in dire financial straits. Their Chartist 'friend promised to help us but he was unable to bring us anything'.

Jones's friend Harney was a member of a left-wing group of Chartists called the Fraternal Democrats, the members of which sought to cultivate contacts with other radical groups. Marx attended an important dinner where Harney was present near the end of 1849.

In his speech at Rochdale in 1877, when he also gave an account of the old stamp system that had restricted newspaper publishing, John Bright was talking primarily about the benefits of Free Trade, one of the other great political causes, like Chartism, that dominated the British scene around the time the Marxes arrived in London. One of the great triumphs of the Free Trade movement was the abolition of the Corn Laws in 1846.

On one level this was a blow dealt by the growing class of the bourgeoisie, represented in Parliament by the Whigs, against the land-owning class, represented by the Tories. The Corn Laws had secured the profits the land-owners made from growing corn by restricting cheap foreign imports. Their repeal was supposed to make food cheaper for the workers, but in a talk on the subject of Free Trade given in Brussels in January 1848, Marx attempted to look behind the promising façade of the Free Trade movement to see what unbridled Free Trade would mean for ordinary people.

The pamphlet that was published after Marx's talk in Brussels revealed the great man's conviction that lower food prices would naturally lead to lower wages, and that the victory of the bourgeoisie that unbridled Free Trade would represent would increase Britain's commitment to something like a pure capitalist system; a callous, inhuman, alienating system that tended to view workers and their labour as mere commodities.

Since Marx felt that this would accelerate the processes that would lead to what he regarded as the inevitable supremacy of the proletariat, he concluded his talk in Brussels by stating that, if given the opportunity to vote in favour of Free Trade, he would do so, on the basis that it was likely to drive 'the antagonism between the bourgeoisie and the proletariat to the extreme. In a word, the system of commercial freedom hastens the social revolution'.

Looking with Marx's eyes, we might be tempted to equate the Free Trade movement of John Bright and others with modern libertarian or neoliberal politics and economics, as seen in the United States and elsewhere, devotees of which advocate the exposure of national economies to unrestricted market forces, in the hope that this harsh medicine might cure various economic and social ills.

If nothing else, Marx's Free Trade talk in Brussels showed that, though he was never a great public speaker, he was still capable of giving a lecture in French, and was very much *au fait* with British affairs even before he came to live in London in 1849.

The Marxes' home in Chelsea (Cody Carvel)

# London at Last

We might think that, with their wealthy and even aristocratic connections, the Marxes might have lived in some style in Victorian London. Not a bit of it. At first Frau Marx lived in a lodging-house belonging to a master-tailor in Leicester Square, but soon the family was attempting to live in rather swish lodgings at number four Anderson Street, Chelsea. This quickly foundered because they simply could not pay the six pounds monthly rent, worth over five hundred pounds today, and also feed and clothe themselves. Located just off the King's Road in fashionable Chelsea, Anderson Street is still expensive – in 2022 a two-bedroom flat sold for over one point three million pounds.

The Anderson Street houses from which such flats are carved are large, well-proportioned three-storey town-houses, with basements accessible via the typical London 'areas', enclosed by railings, and front doors placed at the tops of short flights of stairs. They were evidently designed for well-to-do families with servants. Even when divided into many flats these houses can serve as a sort of three-dimensional diagram of the English class system as Marx came to know it. It was the *Upstairs, Downstairs* world immortalised in the British TV drama series of the same name, the first episode of which aired in 1971.

Food was stored and prepared in the strictly functional, if not spartan, conditions found in the basement, where live-in servants were often expected to sleep in cramped conditions, sometimes in the kitchen itself. Meanwhile the owners lived in spacious, well-lit, well-appointed rooms above, over-stuffed with valuable knick-knacks in the Victorian style, and kept scrupulously clean by the servants, who were themselves stratified according to rank.

The underground lives of servants and others in Victorian cities inspired one element of H.G. Wells's 1895 story *The Time Machine*. Here, in the far future, the underground people have evolved into the terrifying Morlocks, who prey on the innocent surface-dwelling Eloi. Referencing ill-lit, underground work-places, the time-travelling hero of Wells's story asks 'even now, does not an East-end worker live in such artificial conditions as practically to be cut off from the natural surface of the earth?'

The façades on Anderson Street combine the handsome London 'yellow stock brick' above with immaculate white-painted ground-floor exteriors. Among other famous nineteenth-century residents of Chelsea were Thomas Carlyle, Elizabeth Gaskell, Oscar Wilde, George Eliot, Henry James and Dante Gabriel Rossetti.

Though they soon had to move on, the Marxes were in Chelsea long enough for their fourth child and second son, Henry (or Heinrich) to be born there on the fifth of November 1849. In 1847 a son, Charles, had been added to the Marxes' previous children, Jenny Caroline (called Jennychen) and Jenny Laura. Charles, little Jenny and Laura were what Frau Marx called the 'three poor persecuted small children' she had brought to London.

British readers will know that Henry's birthday, the fifth of November, is Guy Fawkes Night, otherwise known as Bonfire Night. This is when we are supposed to celebrate the discovery of a Catholic plot to blow up Parliament, on the fifth of November 1605. Bonfires are still lit and fireworks are let off to to celebrate this event, although there is an uncomfortable anti-Catholic element to the festival. Effigies or 'guys' are made of Fawkes himself, which are sometimes burned on the bonfires, as effigies of the Pope used to be in some places. Before the night of the fifth, children take their home-made 'guy' from door to door, begging for a 'penny for the guy'. American readers might think of Guy Fawkes Night as a combination of Thanksgiving (also a

November festival) and Independence Day, when fireworks are a feature.

The plan of the conspirators back in 1605 had been to blow up Parliament during a visit by the king, James I (not the much earlier James I of Scotland to whom Jenny Marx was related). It was the Yorkshireman Guy or Guido Fawkes who was discovered with barrels of gunpowder in the cellars of Parliament, so the Marxes thought it would be appropriate to nick-name their new boy 'Guido' or 'Little Fawkes'. In her autobiographical sketch, Jenny Marx wrote that:

On November 5, while the people outside were shouting "Guy Fawkes for ever!", small masked boys were riding the streets on cleverly made donkeys and all was in an uproar, my poor little Heinrich was born.

The 'cleverly made donkeys', which are now no longer a part of Bonfire Night celebrations, may have been a custom that harked back to the tradition of parading effigies of Fawkes through the streets on real donkeys. The masks worn by the boys were probably similar to those traditionally put on a 'guy' or effigy of Fawkes as a finishing touch. If the London street boys were wearing Guy Fawkes masks, riding on toy donkeys and shouting 'Guy Fawkes forever' it suggests that their attitude to this failed early seventeenth-century terrorist was quite different to what it was supposed to be, according to the official line. Had they been brought up to admire Fawkes in some way? And by nick-naming their son Guido, were the Marxes tapping in to some old, deep-seated British tradition that reflected a feeling that monarchs and parliaments really did deserve to be blown up?

The figure of Guy Fawkes, and one specific type of Guy Fawkes mask, have become much more visible in recent years thanks to the 1980s comic book series *V for Vendetta* by Alan Moore, David Lloyd and Tony Weare, and the 2005 film of the same name, directed by James McTeigue and starring the Israeli-American actress Natalie Portman. In the comic books, the central character, V, wears a pale, leering, moustachioed Guy Fawkes mask, though he is not a Catholic rebel but a vengeful anarchist intent on bringing down the state. Inspired by *V for Vendetta*, members of the online Anonymous collective, which first came to the public's attention around 2003, have taken to wearing similar masks. Such masks are loosely based on a famous contemporary depiction of Fawkes himself, in an engraving of eight of the conspirators by the Dutch artist Crispijn de Passe the Elder. In the comic book, V has a copy of Marx's *Capital* on a shelf in his secret lair.

Little Fawkes was not alone in having a nick-name. Almost everybody in Marx's circle in London had one, including Marx himself, whom even his own children would call 'Moor', 'Challey' (perhaps for Charlie) or 'Old Nick'. Helene Demuth was not only called 'Lenchen' but also 'Nymmy' or 'Nym'. Because of his past military exploits and his interest in all things martial, Engels was called 'General', while Liebknecht was dubbed 'Library' by the Marx children, because of the stories he would tell them off the top of his head. Karl and Jenny's son Edgar was called 'Mouche', meaning 'fly', while, as we know, their youngest daughter Eleanor was called 'Tussy'. Her older sister Laura was called 'the Hottentot' or 'Kakadku' (the term 'hottentot', originally used for the Khoekhoe ethnic group of Southern Africa, is now considered to be racist). Their mother was called 'Möhme'.

Their use of nick-names such as 'Hottentot' and 'Moor' suggests that the Marxes may have been a little self-conscious about their dark features. This was, after all, the age when some women applied solutions of arsenic to their faces to induce pallor, and even took dilute doses of arsenic to achieve the right mix of white and pink. While today some people go out of their way to acquire a deep tan, Victorian ladies wore wide sun-hats and cotton gloves, and employed parasols in sunny weather, to remain pasty. Swarthiness was associated with dirtiness, peasants toiling in the sun, foreignness and outright evil. The Assistant Commissioner in Conrad's novel *The Secret Agent* is able to take advantage of his naturally dark looks to pose as a dangerous alien, and in George du Maurier's best-selling novel *Trilby*, set in the 1850s, the villain is Svengali, an anti-Semitic caricature of a dark-skinned Jew.

While Henry (or Heinrich, Guido or Guy) Marx arrived in Chelsea by one method, thousands of immigrants, both swarthy and fair, were arriving in London at this time, many of whom would turn up at the Marxes' lodgings in Anderson Street. These included Engels, and Liebknecht, whose memoir of the Marx family is an invaluable source for these years. A less welcome visitor was August Willich, who, according to Mrs Marx, turned up in Karl and Jenny's bedroom early one morning 'like a Don Quixote, dressed in a grey woollen doublet with a red cloth round his waist instead of a belt'.

Here Jenny probably does not mean Don Quixote. The eponymous hero of Cervantes' novel is a deluded old man who wears rusty armour: in 1850, when Willich arrived in London, he would only have been forty years old, and his subsequent behaviour and his outré look is more reminiscent of another fictional Spaniard, Don Juan. This particular Don was a famous seducer who first appeared in a play around 1616, the year William Shakespeare died, and roughly the same time Cervantes published the second volume of his *Don Quixote*.

Willich had played a leading role in an armed uprising in Germany in 1849: his aide-de-camp at the time had been none other that Frederick Engels. In London, in true Don Juan style, Willich noticed how beautiful Mrs Marx still was at thirty-six, though she had already borne four children and suffered much hardship and uncertainty. He set about trying to seduce her, although that would have meant betraying his socialist comrade and fellow-German Karl Marx, the lady's husband and the father of her children. Jenny herself described Willich's efforts to seduce her as his attempt 'to pursue the worm which lives in every marriage and lure it out'. Jenny was perhaps thinking of the worms that eat out apples from the inside, thus ruining them.

While the Marxes were still living in Chelsea, Karl found that he had reasons beyond Willich's attentions to his wife to resent the left-wing German Don Juan. Both men were active in the Communist League, but while Marx felt that the time was not yet right to attempt another revolution to follow the revolutions of 1848, Willich, his allies Karl Schapper and Emmanuel

Barthélemy and their supporters wanted a revolution as soon as possible. This led to a split in the League, and much bitterness, which culminated in Willich challenging Marx to a duel. Marx turned this down, but his hot-headed follower Konrad Schramm then challenged Willich, though Willich was a crack shot and, according to Liebknecht, Schramm barely know one end of a pistol from the other.

It is just possible that Marx would have accepted the challenge of a duel with Willich if August had suggested a different choice of weapons. The French refugees in London had set up a 'sword room', where marksmanship was also taught and practised, in Rathbone Place off Oxford Street. Here Marx would sometimes brush up his fencing. Liebknecht tells us that he 'tried to make up for his lack of skill by impetuosity and he sometimes bluffed those who were not cool enough'. The author of *Capital* was instructed in swordsmanship by Emmanuel Barthélemy.

Schramm and Willich ended up facing each other with loaded pistols by the sea in Belgium, since such duels were illegal in England. Barthélemy acted as Willich's second. News reached London that Schramm had been shot in the head, and everybody assumed the worst. But the bullet had merely grazed the side of his skull, rendering him temporarily unconscious. Barthélemy went on to be the last man to kill another man in a duel in England, and to be hanged in London for two murders, unconnected to any duels, in 1855.

The phenomenon of the revolutionary who knows that in theory the bourgeoisie must inevitably fall and the dictatorship of the proletariat commence, but who, like Willich, is ready to force the issue, is reflected in Robert Louis Stevenson's novel *The Dynamiter*. Here an unnamed, earnest but ineffectual terrorist explains that he knows that 'the burgess, our ruler of today . . . would ultimately bring about his [own] ruin . . . and yet how was I to wait? how was I to let the poor child shiver in the rain?'

When the restless Willich had faded into the background, Marx would have to cope with another German Don Juan who also had a penchant for duels, with whose politics he also disagreed. This was the social democrat Ferdinand Lassalle, whom Marx described, in a July 1862 letter to Engels, as a 'Don Juan cum revolutionary Cardinal Richelieu'. Lassalle visited and stayed with the Marxes in London, though Marx found him both annoying and ridiculous – a waste of time. In his thoroughly nasty letter, Marx followed up his Don Juan remark by complaining of 'the sheer gluttony and wanton lechery of this 'idealist''.

Marx's letter about Lassalle was nasty partly because of its anti-Semitism. That a pure-bred Jew like Marx should have written about a fellow-Jew in this way is shocking. If nothing else, it shows how far Marx had drifted from his Jewish roots by this time. He had married a Gentile, fathered half-Gentile children and could be very critical of the Jews in general, as well as Lassalle in particular.

If Marx had decided to embrace his *Yiddishkeit* while living in London, then he would not have lacked for observant fellow-Jews to contact, or Jewish places to go. In 1850 there were some thirty-five thousand Jews in England, about thirteen percent of whom could trace their ancestry back to less than forty families who had come here after Oliver Cromwell as Lord Protector made it easier for observant Jews to live in England. The Jewish population swelled to around sixty thousand by 1850, partly due to immigration from the *shtetls* of Eastern Europe.

If Marx had decided to start attending one of the London synagogues while he was living destitute in Dean Street, he may have been disappointed. Poor Jewish men were segregated and cold-shouldered in these places of worship, as hard-up Christians were in many London churches and chapels. Many working-class Jewish men preferred to join *chevroth*, small prayer groups that sometimes worshipped in very humble settings.

As well as their own internal class struggle, Marx's fellow-Jews in England also experienced other examples of the social phenomena that Marx observed so keenly from his vantage-point under the dome of the British Museum reading room. As poor Jews poured in from Eastern Europe, many were forced to take up low-paid, unskilled jobs in factories, in London and elsewhere. A Jewish proletariat was therefore developing, and as they grew in political self-awareness, they joined or formed unions and became involved in industrial disputes. The short-lived Hebrew Socialist Union was founded in 1876.

A couple of years after Marx wrote his letter about his flamboyant, unwanted guest, Lassalle arranged to marry a lady called Helene von Dönniges, but she was persuaded to defect back to a man to whom she had previously been engaged. Lassalle challenged his rival, a Wallachian prince, to a duel with pistols. The prince shot Lassalle in the abdomen, and he died three days later. In 1875, Marx would mention Lassalle's continuing (and to Marx, malign) influence on social democrat parties in Germany in his *Critique of the Gotha Programme.*

Karl Marx may have thought that he would be able to keep his head above water, financially, while paying a high rent in Chelsea, thanks to the hoped-for profits from a new newspaper, the *Neue Rheinische Zeitung. Politisch-ökonomische Revue.* By the end of 1849 this snappily-titled organ had acquired a publisher in Hamburg: one of the signatories to the contract was Konrad Schramm, who, as we have seen, also showed that he was prepared to lay down his life for his friend Karl Marx.

In our modern age of digital communications the idea of writing and editing a German-language newspaper, published in Hamburg, from London, would not seem outlandish. In Marx's day all the articles, monies and business correspondence had to be sent by post, in hard-copy form, or delivered by hand by people who happened to be travelling between London and Hamburg. The copy for articles could not even be type-written: the first typewriters were not to appear for another seventeen years. One of the problems that contributed to the *Revue*'s demise after only six issues was the printer's difficulty interpreting Marx's scrawly handwriting.

As well as Marx, articles for the *Revue* were written by Engels, Karl Blind (who had met Frau Marx on her arrival in London), the Marxes' friend Joseph Weydemeyer and others. According to Jenny, great effort and expense had been put into the setting up of the *Revue*, which was 'a great success' at first, but failed because Schuberth and Co., the Hamburg publisher, which was also a bookseller, was 'bought over by the German Government' and was 'so negligent and inefficient over the business side of [the *Revue*] that it was soon obvious that it could not go on for long'.

In May 1850 Frau Marx wrote a heart-breaking letter to Weydemeyer in Frankfurt, begging him 'to send us as soon as possible any money that has been or will be received from the *Revue*. We need it very, very much'. 'One cannot say,' she went on, 'whether the delays of the bookseller or of the business managers or acquaintances in Cologne or the attitude of the Democrats on the whole were the most ruinous'. 'Ruinous' meant that the Marxes had put their last pennies into the *Revue*, and were now penniless.

In those days before supermarkets, and home fridges and freezers, when the big weekly or fortnightly grocery shop was impossible, food had to be consumed close to the day it was bought, and middle-class families like the Marxes tended to get food delivered to their doors by local bakers, butchers, green-grocers, fruiterers, milkmen and the like. In Anderson Street, the Marxes soon got into debt with such tradesmen, and the situation became worse when the housekeeper (presumably a housekeeper for the whole building) claimed that the Marxes also owed her five pounds (they had understood that they would only have to pay her employer, the landlord).

Two bailiffs arrived and, according to Jenny's account, 'sequestrated all my few possessions—linen, beds, clothes—everything, even my poor child's cradle and the best toys of my daughters, who stood there weeping bitterly'. The bailiffs threatened to take everything else in two hours, unless some money could be found. The situation offered the loyal Konrad Schramm another opportunity to be injured in the cause. Hurrying off to get help, he jumped into a cab, but the horses bolted. To save himself, he threw himself out of the cab, and returned to Anderson Street bleeding.

A last-minute injection of money meant that the Marxes could sell their beds instead of losing them to the bailiffs. By this time, 'the chemist, the baker, the butcher and the milkmen' were clamouring for payment, and had to be paid off. The beds that were to be sold were put onto a cart in the street, but the landlord appeared, concerned that the Marxes might be trying to sell some of *his* property. The altercation in the dark street drew a crowd of 'two or three hundred persons . . . the whole Chelsea mob'.

The Marxes found temporary shelter in the German Hotel at number one, Leicester Street, Leicester Square (this should not be confused with one, Leicester Square, which is a different building altogether, also a hotel). The building that once housed the German Hotel is still a hotel (now called simply One Leicester Street) with a public restaurant on the ground floor, and from the outside it still looks much as it must have appeared when the Marxes were there.

It lies in a street just off Leicester Square, and has a dark, plain but elegant Georgian brick exterior, with some well-proportioned windows. The façade is now adorned with large white letters advertising 'LANGOUSTE, HUITRES, MOULES' in French (lobster, oysters and mussels). When the awnings are down in warm weather, shading the guests sitting out in the street, One Leicester Square looks like yet another of those English restaurants that try to mimic Parisian ones. This continental influence is nothing new: in the nineteenth century, the area around the Square included a number of foreign-owned hotels like the German Hotel, including Brunet's, Jaunay's, the Cavour and the Sablonière; the last named after a celebrated Parisian chef. In his 1867 book *Curiosities of London*, John Timbs quoted an earlier author who claimed that even in the eighteenth century the whole parish was so full of French people 'that it is an easy matter for a stranger to imagine himself in France'.

In his 1908 novel *The Man Who Was Thursday* G.K. Chesterton confirmed that the area still seemed oddly foreign in his day:

It will never be known, I suppose, why this square itself should look so alien and in some ways so continental. It will never be known whether it was the foreign look that attracted the foreigners or the foreigners who gave it the foreign look . . . as he turned that corner, and saw the trees and the Moorish cupolas, he could have sworn that he was turning into an unknown Place de something or other in some foreign town.

In Chesterton's novel, the hero, Syme, is about to attend what he takes to be an anarchist breakfast held on a balcony overlooking the Square. One Leicester Street has a square black plaque at street level (not a round blue one) commemorating not the Marxes' time there, but the visit of the Viennese waltz composer Johann Strauss the elder in April 1848. Leicester Square itself is now a busy pedestrianised space, a great favourite with tourists, home to cinemas, hotels, restaurants, a casino, a theatre, a Lego store and a shop dedicated to M&Ms, a popular multi-coloured chocolate-coated sweet.

In 1851, the year when the Great Exhibition drew thousands of visitors to London, Mr Wyld's 'colossal Model of the Earth' was set up in the centre of the Square, where there has been a garden since before the Square became built up. To make room for his huge globe Wyld, a geographer, had to temporarily bury the Square's gilt equestrian statue of King George I. Like the Marxes, George was another German immigrant, though of an earlier generation. The Square's garden, still a welcome green space, now boasts a statue of William Shakespeare. The Shakespeare statue and the surrounding area are the targets for a bungled bombing outrage in Robert Louis Stevenson's 1885 novel *The Dynamiter*. M'Guire, the would-be bomber, arrives with his time-bomb in a Gladstone bag, only to find that he cannot leave it at Shakespeare's feet because there has been a tip-off and the Square is swarming with police detectives.

As well as Karl Marx, Leicester Square and the surrounding streets have been home to other luminaries, including the scientist Isaac Newton, the writer Fanny Burney and the artists Joshua Reynolds and William Hogarth. Hogarth's house became part of the Sablonière Hotel: his studio, with its fine skylight, served as the hotel's billiard room.

Though the Marxes found shelter at the German Hotel, they could not stay there for very long. After a week the hotel's management, realising that the Marxes would not be able to pay five pounds a week to stay, refused to serve them their breakfast. It is hardly surprising that they could not pay five pounds a week: their Chelsea flat had cost only six pounds a month.

The Marxes decamped less than half a mile north to Dean Street, Soho where they spent what Mrs Marx called 'a miserable summer' in two rooms above the house of a Jewish lace dealer at number sixty-four. In fact they were there from early May to early December 1850. Macclesfield Street becomes Dean Street shortly after it leaves Gerrard Street (now part of London's Chinatown) to the north-west of Leicester Square, heading roughly north-west. Dean Street, a long, straight street, ends when it joins Oxford Street. Part of number sixty-four is now home to a very swish restaurant offering modern Californian cuisine.

Today the street itself is very varied: the oldest buildings are Georgian ones that Marx would have seen, but many have been replaced by later buildings in different styles, of varying levels of ugliness and inappropriateness. There is a supermarket, a bank, a theatre and a sound recording studio, as well as cafés, bars and restaurants, and the famous Groucho Club. There are also two sexual health clinics. At some of the eateries, including the Californian one at number sixty-four, solitary seekers after Marx's London could end up parting with over one hundred pounds just for lunch. They will pay somewhat less at Quo Vadis, the well-reviewed restaurant at number twenty-eight, to which address the Marxes moved in December 1850.

Marx was not the first celebrated figure to live in Dean Street. Horatio Nelson lodged here just before the Battle of Trafalgar, and the artist George Cruikshank was also a resident. The painter Sir James Thornhill lived at number seventy-five Dean Street: in Marx's time the walls of the staircase were still decorated with wall-paintings by Thornhill. Among visitors to the street were Mozart, who played a concert here, and Charles Dickens, who indulged in amateur theatricals at a Dean Street theatre. Other famous names associated with Soho are those of the actors Charles and Edmund Kean, Charles Kemble, W.C. Macready and

Margaret Woffington; the last one of David Garrick's girlfriends. Authors linked to the area include not only Dickens but also James Boswell (the biographer of Samuel Johnson), the essayist William Hazlitt, and the poet John Dryden.

The Marxes, including Frau Marx, who was pregnant again, squeezed into a cramped apartment at the top of number twenty-eight. They had to share this with their faithful and long-suffering servant Lenchen, and a nurse employed to attend Mrs Marx during her pregnancy. Other residents in the house included a cook, some teachers of Italian, and Frederick Engels. The latter soon discovered that he could not support himself in London. He was forced to move north and work in the office of the firm his father co-owned in Manchester. He made this work more interesting by embezzling cash and cheques from the family business, which he posted to Marx down in London, to help keep the family afloat. To guard against the bank-notes being stolen (cash should not be sent in the post in any case) Engels would cut them in half and send the halves in separate envelopes.

Since the nineteen-seventies, one of the famous London commemorative blue plaques has been sitting high up on the front of number twenty-eight, stating (incorrectly) that Karl Marx lived there from 1851. Unfortunately a number of web-pages devoted to the story of Marx in London have taken the dates on the plaque as gospel. Many of London's blue plaques say something about what the person commemorated did to deserve this sign of recognition. This is not the case here. Even Winston Churchill is described as a 'prime minister' on a plaque, Charles Dickens as a 'novelist' and Agatha Christie as an 'author'. When it comes to blue plaques, Marx is in the same category as his slightly younger contemporary Florence Nightingale, whose London County Council plaque does not tell us anything about her achievements.

Despite Marx's attempts to screen visitors using phrenology, at least one Prussian spy was able to penetrate into the heart of his Dean Street lodgings and send a report back home. It is likely that this man's masters would not have been pleased to read a report that stated that the Marxes were living in luxury in London, and that is certainly not what the spy wrote home.

Although today flats in Dean Street change hands for millions of pounds, and just renting a flat here might set you back over ten thousand pounds a month, our Prussian spook reported that the Marxes lived in 'one of the worst, and therefore one of the cheapest, quarters of London'. 'There is not one clean and solid piece of furniture to be found in the whole apartment,' he went on, 'everything is broken, tattered and torn; there is a thick coat of dust everywhere; everywhere, too, the greatest disorder':

In the middle of the salon stands a large old-fashioned table covered with oil cloth. On it lie his manuscripts, books and newspapers, then the children's toys, his wife's mending and patching, together with several cups with chipped rims, dirty spoons, knives, forks, lamps, an ink-pot, glasses, dutch clay pipes, tobacco ash: in one word everything is topsy turvy, and all on the same table. A rag-and-bone man would step back ashamed from such a remarkable collection.

The dust would have been the inevitable consequence of living in a crowded city where there were many smoke-belching factories, and where every building that was heated was heated with coal or wood. In the Marxes' cramped quarters, the dust was supplemented by the smoke and ash from Karl's notorious cheap cigars: 'when you enter Marx's room, smoke and tobacco fumes make your eyes water so badly, that you think for a moment that you are groping about in a cave'.

The Prussian spy evidently thought that part of the problem was down to the disorderly, 'Bohemian' way Marx preferred to live:

He is often idle for days on end, but when he has work to do, he will work day and night with tireless endurance. For him there is no such thing as a fixed time for sleeping and waking. He will often stay up the whole night and then lie down on the sofa, fully dressed, around midday and sleep till evening, untroubled by the fact that the whole world comes and goes through his room.

If the report is true, it must be said that, as a husband and parent in his early thirties, Karl Marx was living something like the life of some modern university students, especially the type who skip lectures, fail to hand in assignments on time and do not need to take part-time jobs to make ends meet. It does not take a doctor to tell us that this is not a healthy life-style. People who sleep during the day and stay awake at night miss out on the healthy effects of sunlight, which usually promotes both physical and mental wellbeing; and in smoggy Victorian London Marx would have encountered little enough sunlight already. If Marx mixed with people who followed the usual pattern of sleeping at night, he may have found himself out of step with them: tired when they were full of energy, and vice-versa. If nobody else among his family and friends was a night-owl, Marx must also have felt lonely at times.

It certainly cannot be said that Marx thrived on his eccentric regime of sleeping at odd times and subjecting himself to long, intense periods of overwork. He was forever going down with one ailment after another, often at the most inconvenient times, when, for example, printers, publishers and collaborators were waiting for a finished manuscript.

In his letters, Marx frequently mentions a recurring liver complaint, eye problems and painful boils that sprang up all over his body from time to time. In 2007 Sam Schuster, professor of dermatology at the University of East Anglia, made a detailed study of the sources and concluded that Marx must have been suffering from something called hidradenitis suppurativa, or HS. The disease can effect up to four percent of the population, and may be genetic. It is exacerbated by long periods of sitting down, and by smoking, but its root cause remains mysterious. There is still no cure.

HS meant that Marx was sometimes unable to sit at his desk – a terrible predicament for a writer. During his last days of work on *Capital*, he was forced to write standing up. The condition is characterised by suppurating sores – hence the word 'suppurativa' that appears in the name. Marx would slash at these with a cutthroat razor, but this is not supposed to improve the condition at all. He took dilute arsenic for the pain, but sometimes stopped taking the poison and 'toughed it out' to keep his head clear.

Marx was wont to compare himself to Job – the Old Testament prophet from the land of Uz, who endures terrible sufferings. That Job was afflicted with what the King James Version of the Bible calls 'sore boils' makes Marx's comparison of himself with this human by-word for patience particularly apt. Schuster has speculated how the condition may have effected Marx's outlook and his writings. Did sore boils lower his self-esteem and make him feel alienated?

Although she was feeling unwell during her fifth pregnancy, Frau Marx decided to visit an uncle of Karl's in Holland to beg for his help. The gamble did not pay off. The uncle was 'in a very bad temper' and evidently did not approve of his nephew's revolutionary activities. He refused to give anything other than a small gift for little Fawkes, and Jenny returned home to London in despair.

Henry, Heinrich, Guy, Guido or Little Fawkes did not last long after his mother's return. He hardly slept, and he began to experience violent convulsions. If his mother was part of the social class that expected her groceries to be delivered, she was also part of the class who expected to be able to employ wet-nurses. This was beyond the Marxes at this time, and Jenny was forced to breast-feed the sickly infant herself. This gave her a bad back, and cracked nipples that even leaked blood into the baby's mouth.

Little Fawkes died at number sixty-four Dean Street in November 1850, of convulsions caused by pneumonia. He was the first child the Marxes had lost. He was not to be the last. In the next month, the family moved along the street to number twenty-eight. Jenny was already pregnant with Franzisca, her fifth child, who also died after a little over a year.

Liebknecht wrote about how members of Marx's circle would sometimes 'relapse' into their 'old student pranks'. One night Liebknecht, Marx and Marx's old college friend Edgar Bauer decided to 'take something' in every bar between Oxford Street and Hampstead Road. This could have turned into an epic pub-crawl, given what Liebknecht described as 'the enormous number of saloons in that part of the city'. In the Tottenham Court Road they were lured into a pub by the sound of communal singing. They were greeted hospitably, but soon the conversation turned to comparisons between Germany and England. Marx began to insist on the superiority of German music, referencing Beethoven, Handel and Haydn, and even throwing in Mozart for good measure, although the composer of *The Magic Flute* was born in Austria.

Liebknecht himself began to compare the political situation in Germany to that in England, stating that conditions in England 'were not a bit better' than they were in Germany. At this point, as he tells us, 'the brows of our hosts began to cloud' and the phrase 'damned foreigners' was heard. The Germans decided to slip away.

They might have done better to demonstrate the charms of German music by singing to the pub crowd. Liebknecht tells us that on one occasion he, Engels and Konrad Schramm 'sung a song that might have softened stones for the delectation of the English regular guests' of a pub 'who rewarded us with a stormy applause'.

Some time after the comrades had fled from the pub on the Tottenham Court Road, in fact at around two in the morning, Bauer stumbled over a heap of paving-stones, and decided to start throwing them at the nearby street-lamps. By the time the trio had wrecked five lamps, four or five policemen turned up, and the 'damned foreigners' took to their heels.

Not the least surprising aspect of this story is that Bauer and Marx were happy to get drunk and silly together, although Marx and Engels had launched a vicious attack against Bauer, his brother Bruno and their circle in their 1844 book *The Holy Family*. Here Edgar was singled out as the purveyor of 'the tranquillity of knowledge' who, in his own writings, had completely misrepresented the ideas of the French philosopher Pierre-Joseph Proudhon, an important influence on the socialists of Marx's generation. Bruno and Edgar Bauer were leading lights of the Young Hegelian group of which Marx had once been a member.

Restaurant below one of Marx's homes in Dean Street, Soho
(Ferran Cornella)

# Life on Dean Street

One can hardly blame Marx for passing the occasional drunken night out with friends: the situation at home at number twenty-eight Dean Street was enough to drive anyone to drink. Although the family somehow found the cash to pay for a wet-nurse for little Franzisca, which at least got the new baby out of their cramped flat for a while, the birth of another child in June 1851 led to much consternation, and the possibility of scandal. This time the mother was not Jenny but Helene Demuth, nick-named Lenchen, the Marxes' loyal servant and companion, but also an unmarried woman, who gave birth to a boy, Henry Frederick Demuth.

There has always been speculation that the boy, who was usually called Frederick or Freddy, was a son of Karl Marx, conceived when Jenny was away in Holland, trying to get help from Marx's uncle. Lenchen would have been twenty-eight at the time, and Marx some five years older. It seems that the child got the name Frederick because Engels, always ready to help Marx, claimed that the child was his.

If Freddy was the son of Marx and Lenchen, then the encounter that led to his conception could not have been one of those classic cases where an innocent young maid is seduced by her master. Marx had known Helene from his childhood – together they had played with the older Jenny von Westphalen – and, in her role as servant-companion in the Marx household, Lenchen seems not to have been down-trodden in the traditional way of Victorian servants. She played chess with the master, and her opinions, political and otherwise, were listened to and respected. When Marx was storming about in one of his angry moods, it was Lenchen who would be sent in to 'beard him in his den'.

If Marx slept with Lenchen, and Engels did not, then all three of them would have known perfectly well that Frederick was a son of Marx – his third (that we know of) and the only one to survive his father, and the nineteenth century, and live into adulthood. It is likely that Jenny knew the secret as well: in her *Short Sketch of an Eventful Life* she refers to 'an event . . . which I do not wish to relate here in detail, although it greatly contributed to increase our worries, both personal and others'. This is supposed to have happened in the 'early summer' of 1851, and could easily have been the birth of Lenchen's child.

There is always the possibility that Lenchen had been made pregnant by someone other than Marx or Engels, but a close look at a surviving photograph of Frederick, thought to have been taken around 1920, shows a man who could certainly have been the son of the author of *Capital*.

The photo, from the archive of the *Spiegel* weekly German news magazine, shows an enviably fit, dapper, moustachioed man in his seventies, whose eyes, eyebrows, nose, forehead and (receding) hairline look a lot like Marx's. The way that the noses of both men turn slightly to the left (from the point of view of the owner of the nose) is particularly persuasive. Marx's youngest daughter Eleanor, whom everybody thought resembled her father, had a similar nose. It is hard to tell how Marx's lips, chin and jaw-line looked when he was an old man, because when he was photographed they were always covered by a thick growth of beard. Frederick's hair and moustache appear white in the photo, as Marx's did later in life, whereas Engels' hair (though not his beard) remained quite dark into old age.

In my opinion, Frederick Demuth did not look like Engels at all. Frederick's expression in the photo is also reminiscent of Marx's, in various photos taken throughout his life. It is relaxed, confident, comfortable and just a little bit twinkly.

The secret of Frederick Demuth's link to Marx was not revealed to the wider family until Engels lay dying of throat cancer in 1895. According to Robert Payne's book *The Unknown Karl Marx*, the way that the (likely) truth was revealed could hardly have been more dramatic, even melodramatic. Unable to speak because of the cancer, Engels, asked about the affair by his friend Samuel Moore, chalked his answer onto a slate. Moore went to visit Marx's daughter Eleanor at Sydenham in Kent, to break the news.

Tussy could not accept this new information at all. She idolised her father, who by this time had been dead for five years, and demanded that Engels retract the accusation. She visited him on the day of his death when, taking up the slate again, he confirmed Freddy's parentage. This scene is well-presented in the 2020 film *Miss Marx*, where Romola Garai as Eleanor conveys her total shock at the news. Somehow the scene manages to avoid melodrama, although the potential for melodrama is certainly there.

According to Payne, Tussy was 'shattered'. She had, however, acquired a brother. This would have been something new for her, as Charles, the last of the brothers she had previously known about, had died when she was only a few months old, long before she could have laid down any lasting memories of him. Payne prints some letters Eleanor sent to Freddy between August 1897 and March 1898, from the home she called 'the Den' at Sydenham, and from Margate, which show that in the years since she had discovered him, they had become very close. On her side, this may have been partly because he reminded her of her late father.

In a letter from August 1897, Tussy confided in Freddy about her feelings for her lover, the reptilian Edward Aveling, from whom she was separated at this point (he had suddenly left the Den, taking much of the furniture with him). 'I have written to Edward once more this morning,' she writes on the thirtieth of August 1897, and goes on:

77

No doubt it is a weak thing to do, but one cannot wipe out fourteen years of one's life as though they had never been. I believe that anyone who had the least sense of honour—not to speak of goodness and gratitude—would answer this letter. Will he do it? I fear he will not.

In the letters, Eleanor also asks Freddy to attend a meeting in her place (he was also active on the left), to look out for Aveling while he is there, and to try to hustle him onto a train at London Bridge, and bring him back to Sydenham. In September Eleanor confides that she is flat broke, 'worse than I ever imagined' and asks for Freddy's 'advice and sympathy'. Other letters reveal that Freddy did lend money to Aveling, and that Tussy is severely depressed, and wondering 'why we go on like this'. 'I am ready to go and would do so with joy,' she writes from Margate in March 1898, but by this time she is back with Aveling, and 'as long as he needs help, I have a duty to remain'. She also reminded Freddy how much she missed 'Nymmy', his mother Helene Demuth, who had died of cancer in 1890, at the age of sixty-nine.

In his Dictionary of National Biography article on Marx, Eric Hobsbawm waxes quite gleeful about the fact that, if Freddy Demuth really was Marx's son, then he was 'the only member of the Marx family actually to be a class-conscious proletarian'. Freddy was a tool-maker, a member of the Amalgamated Engineering Union and a founder member of the Hackney Labour Party. He seems to have lived all his life in Hackney: he was fostered by a working-class Hackney family called Lewis, no doubt because it was considered to be impossible for him to remain with his biological mother, together with the Marxes at Dean Street. Freddy died in 1929, at the age of seventy-seven, having fathered a son of his own, who gave him three grand-children.

Hobsbawm repeats a story about Freddy being paid a substantial sum of money, probably in the mid nineteen-twenties, by the USSR, in return for his silence about his paternity. Later, in 1934, Joseph Stalin is supposed to have ordered that documents relating to the truth about Demuth 'should stay buried in the archive'.

The author of the DNB article on Marx suggests that it was the 'intolerable pressure' of life in Dean Street that 'led to the birth of Helene Demuth's son'. Driven almost crazy with stress, Marx was driven into the arms of the faithful family servant (or perhaps the stressed Lenchen was driven into the arms of her employer).

Hobsbawm's account suggests that, if they really did sleep together, the minds of both Marx and Lenchen were too clouded by stress and frustration to have any worthwhile thoughts. If Marx was able to think at all, we must ask, 'What was he thinking?' Perhaps, as a Jew, he was thinking of the Old Testament patriarch Abraham, who fathered a child by his wife's servant Hagar. The situation was, however, very different back then. After years of marriage, Abraham's wife had remained childless, and she was desperate to fulfil God's prophecy that her husband would be the father of a great nation. When Ishmael, Abraham's son by Hagar, made his entrance, he was banished along with his mother. By contrast, Lenchen stayed put in Dean Street while her son was, in effect, banished. One aspect that does make the biblical story similar to the story of Freddy Demuth's origin is the fact that Sarah, Abraham's wife, was always considered to be beautiful, just like Frau Marx.

Faced with the dire poverty the Marxes suffered in Dean Street, some people would be driven not to drink or ill-advised sex but into gainful employment. Hobsbawm suggests that Marx always had 'a cavalier attitude to the problems of earning a living and to the relation between income and expenditure' which, in London, led to a 'daily Dickensian struggle with butchers, bakers, landlords, and pawnbrokers'.

This brings to mind the character of Wilkins Micawber in Charles Dickens's novel *David Copperfield*, which began publication as a serial in the year Marx came to live in London, and was first brought out in book form in 1850. Micawber is a poverty-stricken family man, although he is evidently also a man of some education and culture, able to employ long words and complex sentences. Like the Marxes, the Micawbers rely on money gained by pawning Mama's family heirlooms.

Unlike Marx, Wilkins Micawber understands 'the relation between income and expenditure': one of his most famous remarks states that, if one's income is twenty pounds a year and one's annual expenditure is slightly less, the result is 'happiness'. With the same income but excess expenditure of just six pence, the result is 'misery'. Like Jenny Marx, Mrs Micawber is determined that she will stick by her man, though there is no suggestion that Micawber is ever unfaithful.

Dickens's character was badly misrepresented in the 2019 UK film *The Personal History of David Copperfield*, directed by Armando Ianucci. As played by the Scottish actor Peter Capaldi, Micawber is incompetent and work-shy. In fact, Dickens's character is desperate to work, always hoping that something in the way of employment will 'turn up', and he does well when given a fair chance in his new life in Australia.

Karl Marx was not work-shy, but he would probably have been unsuited to regular employment of the nine-to-five type, not least because he spent a great deal of time and effort on work that he thought was of European, even global, importance, but which brought in little or no income. Even the Prussian spy who penetrated into the heart of the Marxes' lodgings on Dean Street recognised that Karl worked 'day and night with tireless endurance', though not all the time.

An important task that Marx set himself in those early years in London was the fight-at-a-distance for justice for eleven members of the Communist League who were being tried in Cologne. They had been arrested, then incarcerated for a shocking eighteen months, before their case even came to trial. According to both Marx and Engels, after nine months the authorities decided to prolong the prisoners' time under lock and key *because there was insufficient evidence against them*. Just three months later, the evidence had grown to such proportions that the public accuser asked for more time to assimilate it. There were more delays when the Chief of Police, a man called Schulz, fell ill. When he 'fortunately' died, as Marx wrote in his 1852 pamphlet *Revelations Concerning the Communist Trial in Cologne*, 'the government had to bring up the curtain' on the trial itself.

Marx's *Revelations*, Engels' account written for an American newspaper, and a letter from Marx, Engels and two other comrades that was sent to an English newspaper revealed that much of the evidence brought against the accused in Cologne was forged, and badly forged at that. An item purporting to be a book of minutes of communist meetings in London, stolen from a member of the Communist League, used the wrong first names for many of the comrades, included the minutes of meetings that took place on the wrong day, and contained notes of speeches made in London by people who could not have been in the capital at the time. The forged document also featured minutes supposedly taken down by a man who could barely write.

Throughout the trial, the authorities confused the activities and aims of the communists loyal to Marx with those of the group centred around August Willich and Willich's friend Karl Schapper. In his *Revelations*, Marx reiterated that whereas his group believed that the right kind of revolution might have to be delayed for up to fifty years 'of civil wars and national struggles' while the proletariat prepared themselves for political power, the Willich-Schapp group cried 'either we seize power at once, or else we might as well just take to our beds'.

In the event, the dishonesty and clumsiness of the prosecution case cut little ice. Seven of the eleven defendants were sentenced to prison terms, some lasting up to six years. A young defendant called Roland Daniels was acquitted, but died three years later because of tuberculosis contracted during his long pre-trial detention.

According to Marx, the sentencing of the eleven came about partly because the case was heard by a jury that was 'quite unprecedented in the annals of the Rhine Province'. In this jury 'every one of the ruling classes in Germany was represented and only these classes were represented'. 'With this jury,' Marx went on, 'the Prussian government, it seems, could stop beating about the bush and make the case into a political trial pure and simple'.

One purpose of both Marx and Engels' writings on the Cologne Communist trial was to show that their group was not a band of violent conspirators; but a more patient, watchful, reflective, studious body. Marx had to repeat the performance in 1860, in reply to a pamphlet published in Geneva in 1859, by the scientist and politician Karl Vogt. In his *Trial Against the Allgemeine Zeitung* Vogt had defamed Marx's group, although by this time the Communist League had been disbanded for several years – Marx himself had closed it down in 1852, in the aftermath of the Cologne Communist Trial.

Among other accusations, Vogt described Marx and his followers as blackmailers, counterfeiters and conspirators who were secretly in league with the police. Vogt also asserted that Marx was the author of an anonymous German political pamphlet called *A Warning* that had accused him, Vogt, of being in the pay of the French. Marx's Chartist friend Ernest Jones, who had been raised in Germany and could therefore read German, was among those who were scandalised by Vogt's accusations, believed that they were potentially very harmful, and recommended some form of retaliation. He wrote to Marx:

I have read a series of infamous articles against you in the *National-Zeitung* and am utterly astonished at the falsehood and malignity of the writer. I really feel it a duty that every one who is acquainted with you, should, however unnecessary such a testimony must be, pay a tribute to the worth, honour and disinterestedness of your character. ... Permit me to hope that you will severely punish your dastardly and unmanly libeller.

Marx responded by attempting to sue two newspapers who had repeated Vogt's accusations. These were the Berlin *National-Zeitung* and the *Daily Telegraph* in London. In February 1860 Marx's letter to the editor was published in the *Telegraph*, threatening legal action if the paper did not publish 'an *amende honorable* for the recklessness with which you dare vilifying a man of whose personal character, political past, literary productions, and social standing, you cannot but confess to be utterly ignorant'.

Marx followed up his legal efforts with his own short book, *Herr Vogt*, which made short work of his accuser. In this publication, Marx even managed to show that Vogt was in the pay of the French, although he, Marx, had not written *A Warning,* in which that accusation had appeared. In 1870, evidence surfaced that Vogt had in fact been in the pay of the French, and had once signed a receipt for forty thousand francs from the government of Napoleon III.

As well as exposing a French agent, Marx's *Herr Vogt* again displays the author's talent for mockery and his knowledge of the plays of Shakespeare. The chubby Vogt is compared to Shakespeare's fat knight Sir John Falstaff, and Marx uses his analytical skills to prise open cracks in Vogt's case against himself and his comrades. He also draws on independent evidence to show up inconsistencies, in the manner of a sharp defence lawyer cross-examining a lying witness.

During late 1859 and early 1860, the writing of Marx's witty, scathing demolition of Karl Vogt necessitated a longish pause in his work on *Capital*. Back in 1852, his work on his *Revelations Concerning the Communist Trial in Cologne* was combined with attempts to influence the progress of the trial from hundreds of miles away in London. He wrote that all this time and effort meant that he could not work 'for his daily bread', so that 'at any moment' he expected to see 'really horrid misery' overwhelming his family because of his lack of income. He revealed that, while he was writing his *Revelations*, he was without trousers or shoes, and therefore trapped at home. What had happened? Had he pawned his trousers and shoes? Were they being repaired, or was he waiting until another envelope came from Manchester, with money for replacements?

In theory, Marx was earning his 'daily bread' at this time by writing articles for the *New-York Daily Tribune*, a newspaper founded in 1841 (as the *New-York Tribune*). The *Tribune* was quite unlike some of the struggling, short-lived, propaganda-filled German-language papers Marx had previously written for. When Marx started to write for it, it dominated the New York papers, with a circulation of around two hundred thousand. In the preface to his 1859 *Contribution to the Critique of Political Economy* Marx described the *Tribune* as 'the leading Anglo-American newspaper'. He had been recruited as a writer for the *Tribune* by its foreign editor, Charles Anderson Dana, who had met, and been greatly impressed by, Karl in Cologne in 1849.

The deal was that Marx would be paid one pound per article, worth perhaps ninety to one hundred pounds today, or one hundred and twenty US dollars. At times, Marx wrote two articles every week, but on the whole he resented the work. In the aforementioned preface to his *Critique of Political Economy* Marx remarked that 'the imperative necessity of earning my living . . . reduced the time at my disposal': he would have preferred to dedicate all his time to studying the subject of political economy. Writing for the *Tribune* 'necessitated an excessive fragmentation of my studies'. Although Marx thought this international journalism was a waste of time, his friend Engels mentioned it among his greatest achievements, in his speech at Marx's funeral in 1883.

Marx chafed under the burden, but his arrangement with what may have been the biggest-selling newspaper in the world at that time would have been a sweet gig for any number of London intellectuals, especially if they were freelance journalists who wrote for, and were paid by, other papers and magazines. Marx was even allowed to pontificate and pass judgement on the individuals, groups and indeed countries he wrote about, although eventually the *Tribune*'s editor, Horace Greeley, began to feel that Marx's approach was inappropriate. In any case, it is astonishing to reflect that an American paper with such a wide readership, headquartered near the business district of New York, one of the foci of global capitalism, was publishing articles by *Karl Marx*, sometimes on the front page.

Hundreds of pieces appeared in the *Tribune* under Marx's byline from 1852 to 1861, though a number of these were either written or co-written by Engels. The end of Marx's article on the budget introduced by English Chancellor of the Exchequer Benjamin Disraeli in December 1852 shares a large broadsheet page with a report from 'London John Bull' on mysterious bulk purchases of corn, news from Berlin on plans to repair the Church of the Holy Sepulchre in Jerusalem, an account of a yellow-fever outbreak in Haiti, and news of a new newspaper called *The Intelligencer* that was to be run by and for members of the Chickasaw nation of Native Americans.

Many of Marx and Engels' *Tribune* articles have entered the canon of important works by the pair, are re-printed in anthologies, and are referenced in books on Marx and Marxism. Some of the *Tribune* article were quickly re-printed in other newspapers and magazines, some translated into other languages. Some were extensions of or second thoughts on subjects Marx and Engels had tackled elsewhere, and the contents of some articles were incorporated into books or pamphlets.

So far in this book, we have mentioned a *Tribune* article about Palmerston, others about the Chartists and corruption in British elections, and Engels' article for the New York paper about the Cologne Communist trials, which appeared under Marx's byline. Marx's account of Ann Sandry, a Londoner who died of starvation, appeared in the *Tribune* issue of March the fifteenth, 1853.

Marx and Engels wrote about a wide range of Old World matters in their articles for the New York paper. The only places they usually excluded were Africa, Japan and the continents of the New World. As well as producing material on Britain (including Ireland) and the rest of Europe, they tackled events in Turkey, China, India, Iran and Afghanistan. Marx's writings on India in particular demonstrate his awareness that London, where he now lived, was not just the capital of England – it was the nerve-centre of a vast exploitative empire.

A rare example of Marx writing about America for his American paper is an October 1861 article on *The American Question in England*. This was prompted by a letter sent by Harriet Beecher Stowe (author of *Uncle Tom's Cabin*, 1852) to Lord Shaftesbury, the reforming Tory politician and philanthropist. Marx's article was written just a few months into the American Civil War, and it criticises British support for the rebellious southern states, which seems to Marx to look 'rather strange on the part of people affecting an utter horror of Slavery'. True, Marx concedes, the war was not being fought because of slavery, but the southern states had rebelled because they wanted to continue to enslave people of African origin or heritage.

Marx brought the slavery issue back to his new home, Britain, in a *Tribune* article of February 1853. This concerned the Duchess of Sutherland, who was president of an assembly that took place at Stafford House in Bloomsbury. The duchess's assembly of concerned ladies called upon 'their sisters' in America to reject slavery. This, Marx implied, was an example of gross hypocrisy, since the duchess and her forbears had treated what Marx calls 'the Scotch-Gaelic population' of their Scottish lands with oppressive cruelty. They had perverted the old clan system, transforming 'ancient tribute' into extortionate demands for money, so that the head of the clan could finance his life-style, 'entangled in the dissipation of the Court of London'.

After 1811 the Countess of Sutherland started to turn over her vast Scottish estates to grazing for sheep. The human inhabitants, who by then numbered some fifteen thousand, were brutally expelled, as part of what became known as the 'highland clearances':

From 1814 to 1820, these 15,000 inhabitants, about 3,000 families, were systematically expelled and exterminated. All their villages were demolished and burned down, and all their fields converted into pasturage. British soldiers were commanded for this execution, and came to blows with the natives. An old woman refusing to quit her hut was burned in the flames of it. Thus my lady Countess appropriated to herself 794,000 acres of land, which from time immemorial had belonged to the clan.

Marx concludes that a woman who had presided over such an atrocity could not plead against slavery, any more than a Manchester cotton lord, or the Duke of Atholl, who had turned land that had once fed the people into forests filled with game, for sport.

Anyone with a knowledge of Irish history will know that the British did something similar there, over many generations. In another 1853 *Tribune* article Marx laid bare the abuses of Ireland's notorious absentee British landlords, and even quoted from the anti-socialist philosopher Herbert Spencer. In his book *Social Statics*, published in 1851, Spencer had argued, remarkably, that all private ownership of land, anywhere on the planet, should be abolished, and that, in effect, land should be nationalised. Under Spencer's proposed system, 'instead of leasing his acres from an isolated proprietor, the farmer would lease them from the nation'.

Marx's *Tribune* article on the Duchess of Sutherland includes many of the characteristics of his writing from this time, whether journalistic or otherwise. Here he shows himself willing to draw arguments from remote history, and also from obscure studies penned by forgotten experts, some of which gave him the statistics he included. This shows how Marx could exploit the resources of the British Museum library, where he spent so much of his time.

The Sutherland article also shows up Marx's tendency to try to fit events into historical categories, so that for instance the old clan system that the modern Sutherlands had betrayed is identified as an example of a state of society that preceded feudalism: the *patriarchal* phase. Here Marx also airs his theory that, as society evolves, 'the British aristocracy, who have everywhere superseded man by bullocks and sheep, will, in a future not very distant, be superseded, in turn, by these useful animals'.

There is a hint in the Sutherland article that Marx might be looking back at the old Scottish clan system with rose-tinted spectacles, suggesting that those ancient chieftains might have hit on a way of organising their communities to maximise support for, engagement with and protection of all the members of their clan, who, Marx reminds us, were all related.

This tendency to look for utopias in the distant past reappears in, for instance, Marx's preparatory notes for his *Contribution to the Critique of Political Economy* (1859). In notes published as

*The process which precedes the formation of the capital relation or of original accumulation* Marx describes a pre-capitalist type of society similar to that that he thought existed in the old clan days in Scotland. Here clan-like 'tribes', which have evolved naturally from combinations of families, work for the common good, and everybody has a status apart from their work function – in modern terms, they are able to live as 'well-rounded people'. This contrasts with the circumstances of people under capitalism, where they find themselves defined as workers first and foremost, and are only valued as such. Similar 'golden age' ideas appear in Engels' *Condition of the Working Class in England*, and Benjamin Disraeli's novel *Sybil*, which was published in the same year, 1845.

Marx's article on the Duchess of Sutherland was unlikely to endear her to that lady, but another Scot, the diplomat, publisher and politician David Urquhart, befriended the struggling German after he (Marx) wrote some articles, inspired by Urquhart's own writings, about what seemed to both of them to be the unhealthy relationship between the British government and Russia. Palmerston, who was then Home Secretary, and whom both Marx and Urquhart hated, was particularly implicated: was he in league with the Russians?

In a footnote in his book on Karl Vogt, Marx wrote about how he had delved into the history of Anglo-Russian relations and (he thought) had discovered that the secret bond between the Russian tsars and the British monarchs started long before Palmerston:

In digging at the British Museum into diplomatic manuscripts, I came upon a series of English documents going back from the end of the eighteenth century to the time of Peter the Great, which revealed the secret and permanent collaboration of the Cabinets at London and St. Petersburg, and that this collaboration dated from the time of Peter the Great [who died in 1725].

While Marx agreed with Urquhart about Palmerston, and about alleged secret links between Russia and Britain, and was happy to accept journalistic work and payment from the Scot, the German was quite aware that the his new friend was a bit odd, to say the least. In his biography of Marx, Isaiah Berlin calls Urquhart an 'eccentric figure, a picturesque survival from a more aristocratic age', and in letters to Engels Marx described him as a 'monomaniac', and just a plain 'maniac'.

46 Grafton Terrace

# In Suburbia

The reason why the German Social Democrat Ferdinand Lassalle was able to stay (rather too long) with the Marxes in 1862 was that by this time the family had moved out of Dean Street to larger premises at number nine Grafton Terrace, Fitzroy Road, Kentish Town (now forty-six Grafton Terrace).

The move was made possible because in 1856 Jenny had inherited family monies adding up to two hundred and seventy pounds, equivalent to perhaps twenty thousand today. As Jenny wrote, this allowed them to pay their debts to 'the baker, butcher, milkman, grocer and greengrocer' and to redeem their 'silver, linen and clothes from the pawnbroker's'. The new house was theirs for a rent of thirty-six pounds a year, plus annual rates of twenty-four pounds (rates were local government taxes: the modern English equivalent is the council tax).

This street of terraced houses is little changed, at least from the outside, since the Marxes moved in. Like the rather larger houses in Anderson Street, these have railed-off 'areas' designed to admit light into subterranean kitchens. Because the family shared a ground floor bow-window (incorporating doors) with their next-door neighbours, they reached their front door via a curved, bridge-like staircase that is most unusual. Running along the outside of the house between the first and second floors is a balcony with a stone parapet, and on the next two floors, round-arched windows face the street. All the houses have back gardens, some now with large, mature-looking trees. In 2023, a three-bedroom flat in the street was on offer for close to a million pounds. A whole house in this street might sell for twice that today. There is no plaque or anything else on the Marxes' old house to indicate that one of the most influential men in the history of the planet once lived here with his family.

Thousands of Brits still live in Victorian or Edwardian terraced houses like the Marxes' new home in Kentish Town. These homes come in all shapes and sizes, from the classic back-to-back two-up-two-down to large town-houses; the nineteenth-century equivalents of the houses in Anderson Street, Chelsea where, it turned out, the Marxes could not afford to live.

Many larger Victorian terraces have whimsical architectural touches designed by the original architects to appeal to the bourgeois tastes of potential buyers, who were often looking for something distinctive, if not distinguished. Where the Marxes had their balcony, arched windows and curved staircase spanning the area, many similar houses have arches in unexpected places inside, crenellated tops to the front elevation, ornate stonework around the front door, or fancy brickwork.

Over generations, the larger Victorian terraces have been extended and otherwise modernised, and some have been broken up into separate flats for generations (look out for multiple door-bells with the occupants' names next to them). Some proud owners decide to reverse decades of modernisation and return their homes 'to their former glory'. This involves such projects as taking out plain false ceilings to reveal elaborate stucco mouldings, fitting sash windows, and even installing wood-burning stoves.

The stone parapet and the drawbridge-like stairs to the front door make the Marxes' new home on Grafton Terrace look a bit like a castle, but to Jenny their 'attractive little house' was 'like a palace for us in comparison with the places we had lived before'. The household consisted of Marx and Jenny, their daughter Jennychen, who had her twelfth birthday in 1856, her sister Laura, who was a year younger, and the new arrival Eleanor, born in 1855. By the time the family moved to Kentish Town, their siblings Guido, Franziska and Edgar had all died. Edgar, whom they lost in 1855 when he was only six years old, had been named after Jenny's brother.

Edgar had always been sickly, and was described by Liebknecht as a 'true child of sorrow'. Both Liebknecht and Jenny believed that if he could have enjoyed some time in the fresh air of the countryside, or by the sea, he might have lived. The new house was near what Jenny described in her 1861 letter to Luise Weydemeyer as 'beautiful Hampstead Heath'. Perhaps a few sunny days up there might have done Edgar as much good as a trip to the country or the sea-side. He was Marx's last (legitimate) son to survive infancy, and Karl was devastated by the loss.

The Marxes and their three surviving children, all daughters, were joined by the faithful Helene Demuth, and in 1857 by a relation of Helene's called Marianne Kreuz. As Rachel Holmes points out in her important 2014 biography of Marx's daughter Eleanor, the Marxes could not have afforded a new servant at this time: it seems that the family were sheltering Marianne so that she could conceal a pregnancy. In 1862 poor Marianne died of a heart complaint, and, as was not unusual at the time, her body had to be kept at Grafton Terrace until it could be buried.

In 1857 Jenny gave birth to a seventh child, whom she said 'lived only long enough to breathe a while and then be carried to join its brothers and sisters'. This latest bereavement and the death of Marianne Kreuz were not the only things to cast shadows over the Marxes' time at Grafton Terrace. Also in her 1861 letter to Luise, Jenny explained how she had to shell out forty pounds to furnish their 'princely dwelling', despite the fact that 'all the linen and other small remains of past grandeur' had been retrieved from the pawnbroker, including 'the old Scottish damask napkins'.

Some of the new furniture was 'second-hand junk', but Jenny 'really felt magnificent at first in our snug parlour'. *At first*. Soon items had to go back to 'uncle's', or 'the pop-house', meaning the pawn-broker, because the Marxes' income was exceeded by their expenditure, and not just when guests like Lassalle were staying. When he stayed, Jenny felt obliged to 'pawn everything that wasn't actually nailed or bolted down' (as Marx put it in a letter to Engels) just to keep up appearances. Perhaps the money from the pawnbrokers was spent on food for the unwanted guest, of whom Marx complained that he 'flaunted his money bags'.

In the same letter in which Marx complained to Engels about his guest in shockingly racist terms, he also lamented the financial woes that had followed the family from Soho to Kentish Town. He owed the landlord twenty-five pounds, and had not kept up with the payments on the family's piano. He had paid ten pounds for the girls' 'wretched school fees' because he did his 'utmost to spare the children direct humiliation' but he still owed money for rates, and also to the butcher, 'not to mention the baker, the teagrocer, the greengrocer, and such other sons of Belial as there may be'.

Part of the problem was that the Marxes were aspiring to a fairly bourgeois life-style; hence the (very poor) piano, and demands for school fees from the South Hampstead College for Ladies. Another problem was that with the onset of a trade crisis in the U.S. in 1857, the *New York Daily Tribune* was no longer prepared to pay as much for Marx's articles as it had been: this meant that the family's income from that source was halved.

Charles Anderson Dana, the *Tribune* man who had identified Marx as a likely contributor, was compiling an encyclopaedia for which Marx occasionally wrote articles, but the income from this work was irregular and unreliable. Dana regarded Marx as an expert on military matters, about which he knew comparatively little, and repeatedly commissioned him to write encyclopaedia articles on martial subjects. Marx had to rely on Engels, 'General', to write these on his behalf, but Frederick was spending far too much time fox-hunting on his fine new horse to churn out the required articles at a useful rate.

Even if they could have lived debt-free, life at Grafton Terrace would still not have been ideal for the Marxes. They were now suburbanites, like Mr Pooter in *Diary of a Nobody*, and although there are benefits to suburban life, there can also be drawbacks. Like suburban housewives down the generations, Jenny felt isolated. In her autobiographical sketch, she wrote that those friends who were still in London lived a long way from Kentish Town, and that in any case the new house was not easy to get to:

There was no smooth road leading to it, building was going all around, one had to pick one's way over heaps of rubbish and in rainy weather the sticky red soil caked to one's boots so that it was after a tiring struggle and with heavy feet that one reached our house. And then it was dark in those wild districts, so that rather than have to tackle the dark, the rubbish, the clay and the heaps of stones one preferred to spend the evenings by a warm fire.

Jenny had been accustomed to leaving the flat in Dean Street to take long walks around London's West End, and with Karl and others she had been constantly attending meetings, clubs and taverns. Without these distractions, she became bored and even seriously ill for a time: what occupied her and made her feel useful and connected was the task of copying out Marx's writings in her own more legible hand.

When the Marxes had lived there, Dean Street, Soho had been a genuine slum, and out in Kentish Town the family still had working-class neighbours. As Briggs and Callow relate in their own book on Marx in London, numbers of workers had been forced to move out to places like this because their homes nearer the centre had been demolished to make way for railways. For many, the choice had been either Kentish Town, the East End or the workhouse.

The hardships the Marxes were soon suffering in their new suburban home were somewhat relieved by the presence of their youngest surviving child, Eleanor, nicknamed 'Tussy'. Growing up, Tussy's only surviving siblings (or the only ones she knew about for many years) were two sisters who were ten and eleven years older than her, respectively. A characteristic of the large, spread-out families of the period was that by the time child number six or seven came on the scene, some of the earlier children might be old enough to look after it, if they hadn't already died, become permanent invalids or left home in search of work.

Eleanor's mother wrote that:

The child was born just as my poor dear Edgar was taken away from us and all the love for the little brother, all affection for him, was transferred to the baby sister. The elder girls fostered and fondled her with almost motherly care. It is true that there can hardly be a more lovable child, so pretty, simple and good-humoured. The most striking thing about her is her love for talking and telling stories. This she got from the Grimm Brothers, with whom she does not part night or day.

Tussy was also very much with Karl: she was his 'real pet and her chatter dispels many of his worries'; and he entertained her with long, fantastic stories spun out of his own imagination. Eleanor's earliest memory was of being carried around on his shoulders, holding on to his black hair, now shot through with grey.

The end of Jenny's description of Eleanor as a small girl hints at the opportunities for a bookish child that were to had in the house in Grafton Terrace. These are emphasised by Rachel Holmes in her biography of Eleanor. Jenny remarked on how the wealth of reading-matter in not only English but also German, French and other languages meant that the Marx children grew up multi-lingual.

It was at Grafton Terrace that Marx wrote his *Critique of Political Economy*, a precursor to *Capital* – in fact much of the *Critique* later found its way into *Capital* itself. As the author wrote in his preface, his *Critique* was partly based on work by Engels and on texts he, Marx, had already written, not for publication but for 'self-clarification'.

What Marx had clarified, to his own satisfaction at least, was that political economy, the subject of the book, was both the basis of, and the key to, what Hegel and others had called 'civil society'. The way that the political economy of a society was organised – its means of production – 'conditions the general process of social, political and intellectual life'. To put it simply, Marx asserted that everything about a society is determined by its means of production: a society where the dominant means of production is agricultural (as in Europe in feudal times) was bound to be essentially different to one where more production took place in factories than on farms.

Marx's *Critique* was published in 1859, the same year as Darwin's *Origin of Species*, and the two books are similar in some unexpected ways. Like the character Casaubon in George Eliot's novel *Middlemarch*, who seeks vainly for 'the key to all mythologies', Marx thought he had found something that might be described as 'the key to all societies'. Supporters of Darwin would maintain that in his *Origin of Species* he had laid bare the key process – natural selection – by which species have evolved over millions of years. Both Marx and Darwin had their supporters and their critics when they were alive, and they still do now.

Marx admired Darwin enough to send him a copy of the second edition of *Capital* in 1873. The great naturalist wrote back from his home, Down House in Kent, thanking the author and expressing his wish that he, Darwin, understood more 'of the deep & important subject of political economy'. He went on, 'though our studies have been so different, I believe that we both earnestly desire the extension of knowledge, & that this in the long run is sure to add to the happiness of mankind'. This is not to say that Darwin read much if any of *Capital*: the copy Marx sent is still in the library at Down House, and most of its pages remain uncut. That Marx sent *Capital* to Darwin has given rise to the myth that Karl asked Charles if he could dedicate the work to him.

In 1860, the year after the publication of the *Critique*, Marx's wife Jenny fell ill with smallpox, although she is supposed to have been vaccinated twice against this dangerous disease. Improved vaccinations, free vaccinations and then compulsory vaccinations had cut down the numbers dying from smallpox in London by 1860, but in that year there were still around fifty smallpox-related deaths in the English capital every week. With the commonest form of the disease, around thirty percent of those who caught it died, and many of the survivors went blind. There was a terrifying spike in smallpox deaths in 1871, evidently brought on by the Franco-Prussian war. As the world saw during the Spanish flu pandemic of 1918, the vast movements of people that happen during a war tend to spread disease.

Back in 1860, Jenny's illness started in the classic way with a 'terrible fever'. Writing to Luise Weydemeyer in 1861, she related that a doctor was called, and that, having examined the patient very thoroughly, he declared 'My dear Mrs Marx, I am sorry to say you have got the smallpox – the children must leave the house immediately'. They went to stay with the family of Wilhelm Liebknecht, while Karl remained to nurse his wife with 'the tenderest and truest care'. Soon the pock-marks characteristic of the disease broke out, and at her lowest point Jenny was utterly prostrated, lying in a cooling draft from an open window, while a fire raged in a nearby stove, and Nurse Marx put ice on her lips and fed her the occasional drop of claret.

At one point Jenny was quite blind, and feared that she would 'remain enveloped in eternal night'. As she got better, she was able to see her children through the window: melancholy quarantine visits where families were separated by glass were a feature of the Covid pandemic in the UK. Like most smallpox survivors, Jenny was left with scarring. She reflected ruefully that:

Five weeks before I had looked quite respectable beside my healthy-looking girls. Surprisingly, I had no grey hair and my teeth and figure were good and therefore people used to class me among the well-preserved women. But that was all a thing of the past now and I seemed to myself a kind of cross between a rhinoceros and a hippopotamus whose place was in the zoo rather than among the members of the Caucasian race. But do not be too terrified. It is not so bad now, the marks are beginning to heal.

It was decided that it would be safe for the children to return on Christmas Eve, thirty-four days after Jenny's diagnosis.

The year after Jenny wrote to her friend Luise about her battle with smallpox, and its resulting battle-scars, the Marxes' finances became so desperate that Karl applied for a job as a railway clerk. He was turned down because of his illegible hand-writing, which very few of his contemporaries could decipher, but in other ways he was quite unsuitable for regular employment. As we have seen, he suffered from long periods of illness, and was in the habit of sleeping in the day and working at night. His commanding presence, manifest intellect and superior education, which seemed to mark him out as a natural leader, may have intimidated anyone he worked under, and his talent for making enemies and alienating people could not have made for a happy workplace.

Life as an adult railway clerk was unlikely to be happy in any case. In his 1878 book *Our Railways*, Joseph Pascoe asserted that whereas junior railway clerks were well-paid, 'the majority of adult railway clerks are the worst paid and the hardest worked of any of their class'. Many earned less than a hundred pounds a year, though they typically worked from nine to six with a half-day off on Saturdays. Some clerks worked their way up into exalted positions in railway companies, becoming, for instance, the well-paid and highly respectable station-masters of large London stations, who wore silk top hats on great occasions and travelled first class. But as a sickly man in his mid forties, Marx may not have had the energy to climb the career ladder in this way.

If by some miracle Karl Marx had managed to secure employment as a railway clerk in London, and succeeded in remaining in post, the course of human history might have been quite different. If the clerking job took up all his time and energy, *Capital* would never have been published, and the work Marx did as *de facto* leader of the First International would never have been done. Socialism, if it survived at all, would have stumbled into the twentieth century with large chunks of its history and its theoretical basis missing, and few would have remembered Karl Marx, the over-qualified German ex-pat railway clerk, who had once written political pamphlets and articles.

Whether Marx's *Critique of Political Economy* or its big brother *Capital* (a big brother born later, which might have intrigued Darwin) have added to 'the happiness of mankind', as Darwin suggested in his letter to Marx, is unclear. It could be argued that Marx's activities away from the library and the writing-desk while the family was still living in Grafton Terrace, and when they later moved round the corner to Maitland Park Road, certainly added to mankind's happiness, if people are made happier when they are listened to, valued properly and treated justly, and have some control over their lives.

In his *Twelfth Night* Shakespeare, a favourite author of the Marxes, famously included a line about some men 'having greatness thrust upon them'. This is not exactly what happened to Marx *vis-a-vis* what is remembered by historians as the First International, but it is close. Partly by being in the right place at the right time, in 1864 the author of the *Critique of Political Economy* found that power, if not greatness, fell into his lap.

In that year, a meeting was held at St Martin's Hall in London, made up of workers from different European countries, intent on forming some kind of international alliance. The hall itself stood on Long Acre, a street in Westminster. Like the Marxes' houses in the suburbs, and the reading room of the British Museum library, the hall was comparatively new when Marx knew it, when it earned its place in labour history.

It had been built as a concert hall in 1847, with a three-thousand seat space for musical performances, and a lecture-hall that held five hundred. This had all had to be re-built in 1860, following a fire. The building was converted into a theatre in 1867, and later became a department store, then offices. It has now disappeared altogether, having been replaced by new flats in the nineteen-seventies. Modern Long Acre is home to Covent Garden tube station – resplendent in shiny dark-red glazed brick – and to various retail outlets, many of them of the chain variety familiar to shoppers all over the world. Businesses that spanned different countries existed in Marx's day – one concern of the First International was to counter what we now call globalisation with an international network of workers.

Marx attended the first meeting of the new group at St Martin's Hall, sensing, perhaps, that any movement it spawned might have 'legs', especially since the version of trade-unionism many attendees espoused seemed to be rather more political than the usual bread-and-butter business of trade-unionism – pushing for better pay and conditions. The new group formed an executive committee, and the German workers chose Marx as their representative. By the time the second meeting of this committee came round, the entire business of drawing up a written constitution had been put into Marx's hands.

The constitution or 'general rules' of the International Working Men's Association (the IWA) as issued was therefore a predominantly Marxist document, committing the members to a struggle for equal rights regardless of 'creed, colour or nationality', and to the overthrow of the then prevalent economic system and its unfortunate offshoot, the class system. The Association was to meet annually, and work to keep members in all countries in communication with each other. Membership would consist of different working men's associations – this was to be an international association of associations, which was one reason why the membership would grow so rapidly, perhaps reaching as many as eight million.

The general rules of the IWA make for rather dry reading – by contrast, Marx's inaugural address to the Association is much easier to digest. In a little over three thousand words, Marx set out what he thought working-class movements should do, how they should do it, and why. The 'why' included the speaker's revelations about the way commerce was burgeoning in England, drawn from his careful reading of newspapers and official reports, skilfully set against data on how working people, the ultimate generators of all this commerce, were benefiting from it.

Marx's Inaugural Address revealed that the workers were not benefiting at all: while British trade had increased three-fold in the twenty years up to 1863, and the number of super-rich people earning the equivalent of over three million pounds a year in modern money was increasing, official reports showed that huge numbers of ordinary workers, including working children, were under-fed, and living and working in atrocious conditions.

What to do? National prosperity, Marx implied, did not lead automatically to better lives for ordinary people – far from it. The workers had to fight to change things. Although the proletarian revolutions of 1848 had ended in failure, since then the English workers had shown what they could achieve by working together. Now the advent of the IWA marked a resumption of the struggle, on an international basis.

Marx's inaugural speech for the IWA was part of his movement into a position of great power over the new organisation. Isaiah Berlin suggests that Marx gained control of the First International because he was 'altogether superior in intellect, revolutionary experience and strength of will'. In the same year that the superior Marx became the leading light of the IWA, he was able to move his family out of Grafton Terrace, round the corner to superior premises at 1, Modena Villas, later called 1, Maitland Park Road. Unfortunately for twenty-first century seekers after Marx's London, the building was demolished in 1900.

The Maitland Park area of London is named after Ebenezer Maitland, president of an orphanage that moved here in 1847, where it was at first surrounded by green fields. After that, the district soon filled up with housing, some of it very modest, and intended for low-paid workers.

The Marxes' new house, which was certainly not of the type that could be afforded by most manual workers, was detached, and rather larger than the house in Grafton Terrace. Here at last each of Marx's surviving daughters could have her own room. There was a garden and a conservatory, and also space for the Marxes' small menagerie of pets, including two dogs and three cats. The family was even able to find room for a party for fifty guests, shortly after they moved in.

Marx himself had a large, sunlit study on the first floor, overlooking Maitland Park. A detailed description of the room as it was in 1865 was written down by the Cuban-born revolutionary Paul Lafargue, who married Marx's second daughter Laura in 1868. The Cuban knew the place well – at times he practically lived with the Marxes, and even had a swing installed in the

101

garden for little Eleanor, who was nine years old at the time of the move.

Marx's study was lined with books – Lafargue estimated that his future father-in-law owned about a thousand altogether – and there were many newspapers and manuscripts in evidence in his study, piled up on shelves and tables. On the mantelpiece were 'more books, cigars, matches, tobacco boxes, paperweights and photographs of Marx's daughters and wife, Wilhelm Wolff and Frederick Engels'. The impression was of complete disorder, but Lafargue insisted that Marx knew where everything was, and had actually arranged everything in a way that made perfect sense to himself, and aided him in the task of writing and researching.

Lafargue may have been being generous to his idol and future father-in-law: in November 1869 Marx and his daughter Eleanor spent three days trying to restore order to his office. Marx wrote to Engels that his work-space had 'become jumbled almost to the frontiers of possibility'. Eleanor was well-suited to the task of restoring order: she was one of the few people who could make sense of her father's hand-writing. By contrast, Engels' office was always in apple-pie order. Lafargue noticed that Marx smoked and worked at the same time, but he used up a lot of matches because he would put down his cigar or pipe, forget it, then have to re-light it.

Marx's apparently chaotic study in the family's last home, further along Maitland Park Road, was lovingly recreated for the 2020 feature film *Miss Marx*, directed by Susanna Nicchiarelli. The horror felt by Engels and others as they begin to pick through piles of books and papers just after Marx's funeral is nicely evoked in the film. They must try to make sense of it all, in order to complete the publication of the whole of *Capital*, working from Marx's notes.

As well as tables and a wooden armchair, in the study at 1, Modena Villas there was also a leather sofa where the master would rest from time to time, and perhaps read a novel. He had the habit of pacing up and down when thinking, which soon wore a visible track on the floor. Engels had the same quirk, and when they were together they would sometimes pace up and down simultaneously. Years later, when the Marxes were living further along Maitland Park Road, the top-hatted socialist H.M. Hyndman was a regular visitor to Marx's office in his last home: here both of them would 'walk up and down on opposite sides of the table for two or three hours in succession, engaged in discussing the affairs of the past and the present'.

Many middle-class Victorian fathers had book-lined studies, some of which served as the nineteenth-century equivalents of modern 'dens' or 'man-caves'. Sometimes women, children and servants were forbidden to enter at all, or during certain sections of the day, when the *paterfamilias* would enjoy some quiet me-time. In theory, clerical fathers could be composing sermons during these times, but in his 1855 novel *The Warden* Anthony Trollope suggests that this might not always have been the case. Here the worldly Archdeacon Theophilus Grantly always repairs to his study after breakfast, sets out some papers on his desk as they would be if he were writing a sermon, locks the door, retrieves a volume of Rabelais from a secret drawer in his desk, takes to his arm-chair and amuses himself 'with the witty mischief of Panurge'.

By contrast, Marx's study door seems always to have been unlocked, and even little Eleanor could come in and play, and interrupt her father, and not feel unwanted. Some of the flashbacks in *Miss Marx*, which concerns the last years of Eleanor's life, show Tussy as a little girl in her father's study. By making her welcome in his work-space Marx was recreating the situation that had prevailed in the Marxes' tiny flats in Dean Street, Soho, where there was no way for Papa to get away from the kids if he wanted to work in private, without leaving the family home. Marx would also hold political committee-meetings in his ever-open office on Maitland Park Road.

The work-spaces of influential people exercise a special fascination. All over the world, a number of them have been kept as the famous occupant last left them, so that visitors can see where some great literary masterpiece was written, a political movement hatched, or a famous painting or sculpture created. The Weimar study of Marx's countryman Goethe is preserved, complete with quill, dark wood furniture and plain scrubbed floor-boards. An 1831 painting by J.J. Schmeller shows the author of *Faust* standing in this study, wearing one of his famous house-coats, supposedly dictating to an amanuensis, but actually looking seriously blocked.

Also in Germany, visitors can view Martin Luther's study at Wartburg Castle in Thuringia. Here the father of the Reformation is supposed to have thrown his loaded ink-well at the devil. In the British Isles, one can see Carlyle's study in Chelsea, and a writing-shed used by the Welsh poet Dylan Thomas at Laugharne in Carmarthenshire; as well as the remains of Alexander Pope's grotto at Twickenham. Left-wing pilgrims who reach Coyoacán, part of Mexico City, can see the study where Leon Trotsky was murdered by the Spanish Stalinist Ramón Mercader in 1940.

Sometimes the work-spaces of great writers are not preserved, but re-created, or even conjured out of thin air. When I was last in Shakespeare's birth-place in Stratford, I saw a lovely desk and book-shelf set up for the playwright, although it is possible that he never wrote a line in his parents' home. Marx's Modena Villas study, described by Lafargue as 'historic', was recreated in the Marx-Engels museum in Moscow. Briggs and Callow reproduce a photo of this 'diorama' in their book on Marx in London. Since the fall of communist Russia this remarkable 'set' has disappeared.

The Marxes' move to their new detached house was not made possible because Marx was now drawing a salary as *de facto* leader of the IWA: his work for the First International was unpaid. The burst of confidence that carried them into the new place was founded on two bequests – from Marx's late mother (six hundred pounds) and his friend the activist and teacher Wilhelm Wolff, nick-named 'Lupus', whose picture Paul Lafargue had noticed on the mantelpiece in Marx's study. Although he had died a modest schoolmaster, Lupus had quietly saved up enough to be able to leave his friend Karl eight hundred pounds, worth perhaps sixty thousand today. Wolff even left a hundred pounds to his Manchester neighbour Frederick Engels.

Marx soon found that he could not sustain life in the new house on the basis of two one-off bequests, however generous. Money worries descended on *chez* Marx again. The profits from the publication of the first volume of *Capital* in German in 1867 were not enough to help: Marx himself had predicted that these were unlikely to cover the cost of the cigars he had smoked while writing it, cheap as those cigars were.

Published in German, in Germany, *Capital* was unlikely to have a big impact on ordinary English readers. The first English translation did not appear until 1887, when its author had been dead for four years. The first volume – the only one published in Marx's lifetime – ran to over a thousand pages, so that even in English it would have looked like a formidable read for, say, a left-leaning railway clerk who was used to reading newspapers, serialised novels, the occasional political pamphlet and perhaps the admirably brief *Communist Manifesto*.

Even Engels, a native German speaker who was usually so supportive of Marx's writings, complained that parts of *Capital* seemed unnecessarily difficult. William Morris, for whom the lack of an English translation meant that he had to read *Capital* in French, also found the book hard going. 'I thoroughly enjoyed the historical part of *Capital*,' he wrote in the socialist journal *Justice* in 1894, but he went on to admit that he 'suffered agonies of confusion of the brain over reading the pure economics of that great work. Anyhow, I read what I could, and will hope that some information stuck to me from my reading'.

The undoubted difficulty of at least parts of *Capital* has led to a whole industry based around interpreting it for the benefit of readers who cannot or will not get to grips with it directly. There are endless 'companions' to *Capital*, as well as heavily annotated editions, books that present carefully-chosen extracts, and others that attempt to summarise the work. Among interpretations of Marx's great book published in English are those by Leon Trotsky (1940) and Eleanor Marx's slippery lover Edward Aveling (1892). Aveling's attempt to persuade Charles Darwin to accept the dedication of his *Student's Marx* is what has given rise to the myth that Marx himself tried to get the great naturalist to accept the dedication of an edition of *Capital*. The mix-up seems to have arisen simply because Aveling accidentally put a letter from Darwin written to himself into a pile of letters written to Marx.

When it was first published in German, not everybody agreed that *Capital* was hard – in England the *Saturday Review* felt that Marx's 'presentation of the subject invests the driest economic questions with a certain peculiar charm', and a reviewer for the *St Petersburg Journal* insisted that Marx's approach:

. . . with the exception of one or two exceptionally special parts, is distinguished by its comprehensibility by the general reader, its clearness, and, in spite of the scientific intricacy of the subject, by an unusual liveliness. In this respect the author in no way resembles ... the majority of German scholars who ... write their books in a language so dry and obscure that the heads of ordinary mortals are cracked by it.

The first foreign translation of *Capital* appeared in Russian in 1872, though the tsar's empire was then very far from the advanced capitalism of Britain. For a free-thinking Russian land-owner, reading the Russian *Capital* in his own book-lined study on his remote dacha, sometimes looking up to gaze through the window at his cherry-orchard, his duck-pond and his stand of silver birches, the steel-and-steam world Marx described may have seemed as remote and alien as Sung dynasty China. Yet it was in Russia and countries further east that Marx's ideas had the most radical effect.

Readers who managed to reach a reasonable understanding of *Capital*, either in German or in translation, and accepted what Marx had said therein, might have closed the book with a certain feeling of bleakness. To view the entire world, or at least the advanced capitalist parts of it, purely in terms of means of production, economic forces and the exploitation of the majority by a tiny minority, is not necessarily a happy thing. Sometimes, when the scales fall from the eyes, the world that is seen more clearly is not a pleasant sight. In particular, the institutions many turn to for consolation and reassurance, particularly the Christian

Church and its various ramifications, might look to a newly-minted Marxist like just another prop adapted to support the exploitative and unsustainable capitalist system.

Whether it was down to the capitalist system or not, in their grand new house, the Marxes' financial situation got so bad that in 1868 Karl was summoned for non-payment of rates. The mood that had made him apply for a job as a humble railway clerk returned. In a letter to Engels he toyed with the idea of living like a simple worker – in 'a purely proletarian' home, which might have been a solution before he and Jenny had had any children, or when the kids were small, but which he felt would now be 'unsuitable'. Luckily, Engels was doing well in business (though he hated it) and could tide the Marxes over.

When this most useful of friends retired in 1869, at the age of fifty, he was able to pay off the Marxes' debts with a handy hundred pounds, and also pay the family an allowance of three hundred and fifty pounds a year, in quarterly instalments. If Marx had obtained a job as a railway clerk in 1862, he could not have expected to earn this much unless he had been promoted into the role of station-master of one of the biggest stations.

Engels moved to London permanently after his retirement, and from 1870 lived at number one hundred and twenty-two, Regent's Park Road, Primrose Hill, a couple of miles from the Marxes. The Primrose Hill house is still standing, and bears a blue plaque which describes Engels as a 'political philosopher'.

Engels' mistress Mary Burns had died in 1863: his new live-in mistress was Mary's sister Lydia, called Lizzie. The third member of the household was Lizzie's niece Mary Ellen, known as 'Pumps'; but various Marxes, including in particular the youngest daughter Eleanor, were always coming and going. Eleanor in particular regarded 'General', who is not known to have fathered any children of his own, as a second daddy. As well as subsidising the Marx family home, Engels also provided financial help to Marx's daughter Jenny after her marriage in 1872, and to her sister Laura, who married the aforementioned Paul Lafargue in 1868.

As a result of Engels' annuity Karl and Jenny, in their later years, were able to enjoy a lifestyle that was far from 'purely proletarian'. In particular there was a great deal of foreign travel, some of it to visit friends and relatives, and, in Karl's case, to be present at political meetings. Karl, Jenny, and their youngest daughter Eleanor, who never married, also took trips for the sake of their health, to spa towns in Britain and further afield. Marx himself even ventured as far as Algeria, thus leaving Europe for the first and only time.

# Keeping Up With the Marxes

Although Engels' generous handouts made the Marxes' lives more secure after 1869, events in the next year endangered the future of the First International, of which Karl had become the unofficial leader. In July 1870 Emperor Napoleon III, who had been so mercilessly ridiculed by Marx in his *Eighteenth Brumaire of Louis Napoleon*, declared war on Prussia. It cannot be said that the war went well for Louis.

The Prussian army was in much better shape than the French one, and in early September Louis was captured after the Battle of Sedan (in the north-east of France). The clash had been disastrous for the French, and Louis' capture spelled the end of his Second Empire. A republican government was set up in Paris, but when it became known that the new administration was suing for peace with the Prussians, the Parisians, backed by the National Guard, seized the city and set up the famous Paris Commune of 1871. The new republican administration, led by Adolphe Thiers, fled to Versailles. Marx's IWA had skin in the subsequent fight – of the sixty members of the Commune's ruling council, fifteen were from the International.

The Commune, which embraced not only Internationalists but also representatives of a wide range of other political and philosophical approaches, only lasted from the eighteenth of March to the twenty-eighth of May 1871. It fell when the French army regained control after *La semaine sanglante* – the 'bloody week' of bitter fighting, during which as many as twenty thousand Communards were massacred.

The fall of the Commune elicited a sigh of relief from the ruling classes of Europe and beyond. Soon stories were being circulated about the murderous callousness of the Communards, and their persecution of the Roman Catholic Church. In a pamphlet, published under the auspices of the IWA less than a month after the fall of the Commune, Marx set out his own view. In *The Civil War in France* he asserted that, far from being crazed killers, the Communards had been too humane in their approach to their enemies. Their kindness and restraint had amounted to a series of tactical mistakes. If they had been more cruel, their fine new republic might have flourished for much longer. All the cruelty was on the other side, the side of the *capitulards*, a deeply corrupt faction led by Thiers, a man Marx derided for his low cunning and short stature, calling him 'dwarfish' and a 'monstrous gnome'.

According to Marx, the Communards' suppression of the churches, and their secularisation of the schools, was just an attempt to separate Church and state, a noble aim that is enshrined, for instance, in the constitution of the United States. The Catholic Church had been the state church of the French at the time (as the Anglican Church still is in England today). The Commune differed from the French Revolution of 1789, which had led to such bloodshed, because that revolution, and subsequent ones in France, merely enhanced the power of the bourgeoisie. For Marx, the Commune was a genuine working-class revolution.

The publication of the first volume of *Capital*, in German in 1867, had brought Marx, albeit belatedly, a certain amount of recognition: his decisive stance in his *Civil War in France* made him notorious. Many now considered him to be a wild-eyed revolutionary and a danger to society. But at least the English were finally recognising the presence of Karl Marx in their midst; a London immigrant whom they had ignored for over twenty years. One consequence of Marx's new-found fame was that his application for British citizenship was rejected in 1874: he was judged to be a 'notorious German agitator' who had 'not been loyal to his own king and country'. How, then, could he be loyal to Queen Victoria?

As the French government clamped down on the remaining Communards, executing some, forcing some to do hard labour, and deporting others to places like New Caledonia, a cluster of islands in the Pacific, thousands of French refugees flooded into London. Many found their way to *chez* Marx, and one of them, Charles Longuet, a Communard and an Internationalist, married Marx's daughter Jenny in 1872. Another, Prosper-Olivier Lissagaray, was engaged to Eleanor for some years; although she was seventeen years younger than 'Lissa', as he was known in the family.

Michael Bakunin

The failure of the Paris Commune contributed to the downfall of the First International. Another contributory factor was the activity of a charismatic, spectacularly unkempt Russian called Michael Bakunin. Slightly older than Marx, Bakunin was a sort of rock-star of the European radical movements, who had spent years touring around to Germany, France, Italy, Poland and elsewhere, involving himself in uprisings and other developments. He had toyed with setting up secret societies – radical conspiratorial groups along the lines of those described by Robert Louis Stevenson in his 1885 novel *The Dynamiter* (Marx and his followers were happy to reveal that, through one of his henchmen, Bakunin had threatened to kill a Russian publisher). Bakunin was also not above putting around a story that Marx himself was the head of such a deadly cabal, and could order the execution of anyone in the world, just with a word whispered in the right ear.

In London, the bear-like Russian attached himself to the International, and tried to hijack it and turn it into a vehicle for his own political program, based on anarchism rather than socialism. At the Hague Congress of the IWA in 1872, the one he attended in his new grey suit from Moses & Son, Marx proposed that the headquarters of the organisation be moved to New York. The IWA struggled on in the New World for four more years, but was wound up in 1776. Also at the Hague conference, Bakunin and his followers were ejected from the International. Old Communist League hands at the Hague, who recognised that Marx was effectively closing down the IWA by banishing it to America, may have recalled how the old man had closed down the League twenty years earlier.

Marx's daughters Jenny and Laura had married in 1868 and 1872 respectively, and the large detached house at one, Modena Villas was now bigger than it needed to be for Mr and Mrs Marx, their youngest daughter Eleanor, their loyal Lenchen and their pets. In 1875 they moved, just along the road, to a slightly smaller but much cheaper house at forty-one Maitland Park Road. This was a middle-terrace town house with three floors and a basement, the whole terrace being gently curved in the style of the famous crescents and circuses of the Georgian city of Bath. The curve of the buildings followed the bulge in the street here, at the northern end of Maitland Park Road. The bulge allowed space for a half-moon shaped shared garden onto which the Marxes could gaze, if they chose to gaze out of their front windows.

Like many Bath buildings, and like the Marxes' terrace in Chelsea, the ground floor was built of stone, but everything above was brick. The windows on the first floor were decorated in classical style, with alternating curved and pointed stone lintels; and a portico supported by pillars with ionic capitals shaded the front door, accessed via a short flight of steps that spanned the area. As at the Kentish Town house, the Marxes had a balcony, accessed from the first floor. One of the regular visitors to the house when the Marxes lived there was the pioneering female physician Elizabeth Garret Anderson: Eleanor was her patient.

The whole block was badly damaged in the Second World War, and demolished in the fifties. There is now very little of the whole road that is not from the second half of the twentieth century. The newer housing on the side where the Marxes lived follows the pre-war building-line, but on the opposite side of the street there are modern blocks of flats surrounded by grassy spaces.

41 Maitland Park Road

There exist some forlorn photographs of the once rather grand crescent-shaped part of the street, taken just before it was pulled down, by Rosemary Matthews. Matthews penetrated to the first floor, and snapped what had been Marx's well-lit work-rooms, one with French windows leading on to the balcony, home, when Rosemary saw it, to a wrecked upright piano with old sheet-music and other rubbish scattered in front of it. It was in one of these rooms that Marx died, dozing in his chair, on the fourteenth of March 1883. This was also the house where Marx's wife Jenny died in December 1881.

In Matthews' pictures the French windows are smashed, the floor-boards bare, and the whole place looks gutted and derelict. A shot of the street outside shows the remains of a once very desirable address, with a collapsed front-yard wall. A workman with a hand-cart is picking over the remains of the wall, perhaps looking for what we would now call architectural salvage. There was a plaque to 'Heinrich Karl Marx' on the front of the house, though a photograph from the nineteen-thirties shows it after it was vandalised. There is now a plaque on the block of flats that replaced these doomed old houses, a block which curves gently inwards as if in memory of the old street.

Though it looks truly grim in Matthews' photographs, at times the Marxes' last address seems to have been a warm and happy place. It was here that the Marxes kept open house on Sundays, a tradition described in detail by Eleanor Marx's friend Marian Skinner. Her account was published in January 1922 in *The Nineteenth Century and After*, an influential monthly literary magazine that had been founded, as *The Nineteenth Century*, in 1877. By this time, Marian had married and changed her surname to Comyn. She found that the attendees at these Sunday soirees, and at other events at the Marxes' house, were very varied, but tended to be on the impecunious side:

Shabby as to clothes, furtive in movement, but interesting, always interesting.

A goodly number had no doubt found their native land too hot to hold them – clever conspirators to whom London was a chosen centre, political prisoners who had contrived to shake the shackles from their limbs, young adventurers whose creed was of the 'if-there's-a-government-I'm-agen-it' order.

Sunday lunch, when it was open house at the Marxes, seemed to go on all day. After years of cooking with indifferent or downright bad ingredients, Lenchen could finally show her mettle with wave after wave of hearty food served in the sub-basement dining-room. For the hard-up political refugees, this was probably the only decent feed they got all week. Marian noted that Helene, whom she described as 'the nice-looking old German cook-housekeeper' who had a fresh complexion and wore gold earrings, was particularly good at baking. For Eleanor's friend, Lenchen's jam tarts remained 'a sweet and abiding memory'.

Marian Simmonds had first come to the house as a member of Eleanor's Dogberry club, which met to read Shakespeare plays aloud together. Named after a comical character in Shakespeare's *Much Ado About Nothing*, the club was supposed to meet in the houses of each of its members in turn, but, as often happens in these cases, one home, that of Karl Marx, a 'very ordinary suburban villa', became the usual venue. The Dogberry was not just a club of enthusiastic amateurs, as we might expect. Among its members was a successful playwright, a published poet and at least one professional actor, Mrs Theodore Wright (originally Alice Austin).

Mrs Wright had played the part of Mrs Alving in an English version of Ibsen's *Ghosts* in London in 1891. The production was very controversial, not least because the play, which touches on themes such as adultery and syphilis, had been banned by the Lord Chamberlain, who then acted as the censor of theatrical performances. Ibsen, whose plays often seek to lay bare the ignorance, hypocrisy, intolerance and philistinism of the bourgeoisie, was a great favourite with London radicals at the time. George Bernard Shaw published his essay *The Quintessence of Ibsenism* in the same year that Mrs Wright portrayed Mrs Alving, and Eleanor Marx learned Norwegian just so that she could translate Ibsen's plays. Mrs Wright was sketched by the artist Walter Sickert while onstage in *Ghosts*.

According to Marian, Karl and his wife Jenny would sit in on the Dogberries' play-readings although Marx himself, the man who had once bellowed lines from Goethe across Hampstead Heath, never read a part himself. Marian thought that this was fortunate, since he had a guttural voice and, still, a strong German accent. But by the time the Dogberries came into being, Marx's lungs were probably so compromised by decades spent chain-smoking cheap cigars that he no doubt felt he wouldn't be up to reading a part well. That he listened in to the readings is hardly surprising. As we have seen, Shakespeare was one of his favourite authors, and Marian tells us that by this time Marx seldom went out in the evenings, so that attending a theatre in London might have been problematic.

After the readings, the company would indulge in parlour games such as charades, and dumb-crambo, a version of charades where a word (not a book or play) has to be guessed at, and in which a word rhyming with the mystery word is given as a clue. Marx enjoyed watching these games:

As an audience he was delightful, never criticising, always entering into the spirit of any fun that was going, laughing when anything struck him as particularly comic, until the tears ran down his cheeks – the oldest in years, but in spirit as young as any of us.

Marian was surprised that Marx had time for such frivolous pursuits – she got the impression that he was working hard, holding in his hands 'the threads of that vast network of European Socialism', beavering away in his 'good-sized, well-lighted' study, 'lined with plain wooden bookshelves and having a large writing-table set at right angles to the window'.

The future Mrs Comyn was not only present at the Sunday open-houses at Maitland Park and the meetings of the Dogberry club. It seems that she would often visit just to be with her friend Eleanor – the two would sit on the heart-rug together, like cats. Marian often witnessed her friend's father setting off for his daily constitutional, at dusk, wearing a long black cloak so that he looked like 'a conspirator's chorus'. Marx's habit of stepping out at night may has been related to his skin problem, hidradenitis suppurativa. HS is often accompanied by inflammatory eye disease or uveitis. Symptoms can include sensitivity to light. Another symptom, blurred vision, may account for Marx's occasional problem identifying which of the houses on the crescent was actually his, when he returned home from his walks.

No doubt some of the attendees at the Marxes' Sundays at home were police spies or, like Mr Verloc in Conrad's *Secret Agent*, were passing information to some foreign embassy in London. For *The Man Who Was Thursday* G.K. Chesterton invented a fantastical branch of the police service that was concerned with checking out precisely the kinds of apparently innocent social gatherings that took place under the Marxes' roof.

The philosophical beat copper who introduces their work to Syme, the hero of Chesterton's novel, explains that whereas 'the ordinary detective goes to pot-houses to arrest thieves; we go to artistic tea-parties to detect pessimists'. This work is necessary because 'the scientific and artistic worlds are silently bound in a crusade against the Family and the State'. Although, as in Conrad's *Secret Agent* and Stevenson's *Dynamiter*, the villains in Chesterton's book are not socialists but anarchists, the link between the worlds of radical science and art is reminiscent of the Marx household, if we regard Marx as a scientist, as many did.

Some attendees at the Marxes' Sunday at homes who were not friends, comrades or spies might have been there out of curiosity, to get a look at the 'notorious German agitator'. Others were curious, but unable to meet Marx in person. One such was the Empress Frederick, eldest daughter of Queen Victoria, who relied on a report from her friend the aristocratic Liberal MP Sir Mountstuart Elphinstone Grant Duff to get some idea of the author of *Capital*. Her imperial highness had once asked this magnificently-named nob if he knew Marx. At the time he did not, but after he lunched with him in February 1879, he sent the empress a full account.

The lunch took place at the Devonshire Club, one of the exclusive gentlemen's clubs in St James's, which closed its doors in 1976. The knight ate with Marx and the philanthropist Leonard Montefiore, a Jew like Marx and a Balliol man like Grant Duff. Like many others, Grant Duff was half-expecting an ogre, 'a gentleman who is in the habit of eating babies in their cradles', but found Marx interesting, harmless and humorous. He seemed to Grant Duff to have 'very correct ideas when he was conversing of the past and the present, but vague and unsatisfactory when he turned to the future'. Among the prophesies Marx shared with his companions over lunch was that of 'a great and not distant crash in Russia'. He asserted that the revolution in Russia would spread to Germany, where Marx believed there was 'much discontent', most notably in the army.

Marx thought that increased spending on armaments was draining the purses of many European nations, which was bound to lead to revolution. Because of this vast expenditure, Germany in particular was going through a terrible crisis, which must lead to the 'really great misery' that Grant Duff thought was a prerequisite for any revolution. Although Grant Duff thought that Marx's ideas were 'too dreamy to be dangerous' he wrote to the Empress Frederick that he agreed with his sense that 'mad expenditure on armaments is obviously and undoubtedly dangerous'.

But if the revolution comes, asked the Liberal aristocrat, 'and you have your republican form of government – it is still a long long way to the realization of the special ideas of you and your friends'. In other words, Marx was being asked, Won't it inevitably be the *wrong kind of revolution*? 'Doubtless,' Marx answered, 'but all great movements are slow. It would merely be a step to better things as your Revolution of 1688 was – a mere step on the road'.

Grant Duff thought Marx looked a little small, physically – surprising when so many people, even at this late date, found him stocky and physically imposing. Perhaps Marx's lunch companion could sense the various maladies that plagued the German in his last years, described on his death certificate as 'cachexy' or wasting away. Grant Duff lunched with Marx just two years before his beloved Jenny died at the Maitland Park Road house, an event that seems to have darkened Karl's whole world. Indeed Engels said at the time that Marx himself had, in effect, been killed by this loss. The morale of the patient was further crippled by the terrible news of the death of the other Jenny, his daughter, on the eleventh of January 1883, at Argenteuil, a suburb or Paris. Jennychen had probably succumbed to bladder cancer. It was just over two months later that her father fell asleep in his chair at forty-one Maitland Park Road. He was sixty-four years old.

As Frederick Engels put it in his speech over the grave of Marx at Highgate Cemetery:

On the 14th of March, at a quarter to three in the afternoon, the greatest living thinker ceased to think. He had been left alone for scarcely two minutes, and when we came back we found him in his armchair, peacefully gone to sleep – but for ever.

What had claimed Marx's life was probably a deadly combination of bronchitis and pleurisy.

Few people turned up to Marx's funeral – perhaps fewer than twenty. It is possible that there was a mix-up and the story got around that Marx was to buried in Paris. Among the mourners were Engels, Eleanor and Aveling, Lenchen, Lessner, Liebknecht and Marx's two sons-in law, Lafargue and Longuet. Just a few days after Karl was buried, Longuet's four year-old son Harry died: he was laid to rest with his grandparents. Lenchen followed in 1890, after working for Engels for some years.

Paul Lafargue and his wife, Marx's daughter Laura, died in a suicide pact in Paris in 1911, when they were both in their sixties. Paul's suicide note explained that he had killed himself to avoid the misery of old age. They were buried at the Père Lachaise cemetery in Paris, also the last home of Oscar Wilde and the rock musician Jim Morrison. All three of the Lafargue's children had died young: today the surviving descendants of Karl and Jenny Marx are all also descendants of the Longuets.

Marx's wife had been buried at Highgate in 1881, which must have seemed a natural choice, since it is so close to Maitland Park. It is one of what are now called the 'magnificent seven' nineteenth-century cemeteries that surround London. The others are Kensal Green, West Norwood, Abney Park, Brompton, Nunhead and Tower Hamlets. These cemeteries had been set up because London's graveyards were so full that some had become a threat to public health. George Alfred Walker, who among other things was a sanitary reformer, set himself the unenviable task of writing a series of exposés of the appalling state of these grave-yards, which were published between 1841 and 1852. One of 'Graveyard' Walker's books, *Burial-ground Incendiarism* (1846) recounted how old bones and coffins were secretly burned to make way for new bodies.

Each of the magnificent seven cemeteries first opened their gates between 1833 and 1841. Highgate buried its first customer in 1839. Although Karl Marx is probably the most famous person to have been buried here, other names include Charles Chubb, the manufacturer of locks and safes, Charles Cruft of dog-show fame, the physicist Michael Faraday, the author John Galsworthy, and various members of the Rossetti family, including the poet Christina.

The most ghoulish story that is attached to Highgate Cemetery concerns Christina Rossetti's sister-in-law, Elizabeth, usually remembered as Lizzie Siddal. Lizzie, a Pre-Raphaelite 'stunner' and a painter and poet in her own right, died in 1862, at the age of just thirty-two. Her husband the poet and painter Dante Gabriel Rossetti placed a manuscript of some of his own poems in her coffin, which was duly interred at Highgate. The coffin was dug up again in 1869 so that Rossetti could publish the poems, once the manuscript had been disinfected and the poems copied out.

Dante Gabriel was not buried here, but Lizzie and her in-laws were interred in the older, western side of Highgate cemetery, which was intended for Anglicans. As their surname would suggest, the Rossettis, like the Marxes, were a family with continental links. Christina and Dante Gabriel's father Gabriele had been born in Italy in 1783. Gaetano Polidori, their grandfather on their mother's side, who later lived and died in Highgate itself and is also buried in the cemetery, had been born in Tuscany twenty years earlier.

The most impressive tomb (as opposed to a mere grave) on the western side of the cemetery is that of the family of Julius

Beer, a German immigrant like Karl Marx, born in Frankfurt in 1836. Beer made money on the London stock exchange (as Marx is supposed to have done, though on a much smaller scale) and built his magnificent family mausoleum, completed around 1878, partly as a last home for his daughter Ada, who died in 1875 at the age of eight. Julius himself, his wife, his brother Arnold and his son were later interred here.

The Beer tomb was designed as a miniature version of the Mausoleum of Halicarnassus (now Bodrum, Turkey), one of the ancient wonders of the world, built for the local king Mausolus between about 353 and 351 BCE. Parts of the ancient Mausoleum are displayed at the British Museum. That such a monument could have been built for the Beer family, who are otherwise quite forgotten and were only ever distinguished by their wealth, is a nice demonstration of some of Marx's ideas. Under capitalism, everything is commodified – everything can be bought and sold, including some forms of lasting fame and honour after death.

The Beer mausoleum overlooks one of the western cemetery's most iconic features, the Circle of Lebanon, a series of tombs with classical-style entrances, built around an ancient cedar which unfortunately had to be removed in 2019. Here both Radclyffe Hall, author of *The Well of Loneliness* (1928) and her lover Mabel Batten sleep the big sleep. Although Highgate is the last home of many arty, alternative and even bohemian types such as the Rossettis and Radclyffe Hall, the bodies buried here are predominantly those of representatives of the bourgeoisie, a class Marx believed would disappear after the final struggle against their opponents, the proletariat.

Although pauper's burials could happen here, there are very few aristocrats buried at Highgate, and no royalty. Such people tend to be buried in family vaults on their own estates, or under the flagstones of private chapels or churches that have been connected to the family for generations. Considered as a representative of the German aristocracy, the presence of Marx's wife's body at Highgate rather raises the tone.

Karl and Jenny were buried in the newer, eastern part of Highgate, which first opened in 1855. The graves and tombs here lack the macabre eccentricity of some of those in the western part, but there is a higher concentration of celebrities, including some who were laid to rest in the twenty-first century. Among Marx's contemporaries are the novelist George Eliot, author of *Middlemarch*, who like Marx was buried here because she was a religious sceptic. This part of Highgate also houses the remains of George Henry Lewes, Eliot's long-time partner.

The religious dissenters' part of Highgate Cemetery sounds like a grudging adjunct to the part set aside for Anglican believers, but in his book *The Victorian Celebration of Death* J.S. Curl asserts that the move away from choked grave-yards to suburban cemeteries was inspired, in Britain, the United States and elsewhere, by the success of Père Lachaise cemetery in Paris, where the Lafargues are buried. Père Lachaise was founded partly because the secularizers of the eighteenth-century French Revolution wanted to detach death and the dead from Christianity, churches and church-yards.

A number of latter-day Marxists, socialists and communists also sleep in the dissenters' part of Highgate cemetery, including the historian Eric Hobsbawm, who wrote the article on Marx that is included in the latest edition of the British Dictionary of National Biography. Among the dissenters is also Sir Leslie Stephen, first editor of the DNB, who was the father of Virginia Woolf.

The grave of a friend of George Eliot lies right opposite that of Karl Marx: that of the Victorian philosopher Herbert Spencer (1820-1903). In his speech over the grave of Marx, Engels called his late friend the world's 'greatest living thinker'. In 1883, when Marx died, many would have disagreed with Engels simply because they believed that Spencer was the greatest.

It is hard to overestimate Spencer's reputation during his life, but from around 1900 people just stopped reading him. In this and other respects he is interesting to compare with Marx, who was just two years older and, as we know, quoted from Spencer in an 1853 article on the Irish question, published in the *New-York*

*Daily Tribune.* While Spencer found fame during his life, which then vanished altogether, Marx spent decades in utter obscurity before his death, yet is now one of the best-known figures in world history. His influence and reputation have even survived the collapse of the Soviet Union.

While Spencer, regarded as a polymath, wrote about every subject imaginable, sometimes all in one book, Marx didn't stray too far from his central interest, political economy and its wide-spreading ramifications. Marx's various physical ailments effected his mood, robbing him of sleep and making him irritable, while Spencer's mental problems caused him to succumb to various psychosomatic ailments.

While Marx could be sociable, had a wife, children, grandchildren and many friends and acquaintances, Spencer felt stranded, lonely and horribly bored in later life. While Marx had failed to find employment as a railway clerk, Spencer had worked for years as a railway engineer. With his spreading beard Marx could look like a bust of Zeus, an Old Testament prophet, or perhaps a hippy guru from the nineteen-sixties; a sort of Allen Ginsburg figure. Herbert's straggly mutton-chop whiskers meant that he never looked like anything other that a studious Victorian gent. Although Marx and Spencer would have disagreed on many subjects, both held to that typical nineteenth-century belief in general development, improvement, progress – in a word – evolution.

One of Spencer's forays into Marx's field, an article called *The Coming Slavery*, published in the *Contemporary Review* in April 1884, elicited a response from Marx's son-in-law Paul Lafargue. Paul's *A Few Words With Herbert Spencer* was published in *To-Day* later the same year. In *The Coming Slavery* Spencer had implied that socialistic reforms such as 'nationalisation of land, banks, railways, mines, factories, and other private instruments of production' would be disastrous, since 'no political alchemy will get golden conduct out of leaden instincts . . . no well-working institution will be framed by an ill-working humanity'.

Lafargue responded by asserting that, if Spencer had understood Darwin properly, he would have realised that the current conditions in capitalist society were bound to give people 'leaden instincts': they weren't that way naturally. In a foot-note to his article Lafargue drew attention to 'Mr. Spencer's deplorable and inveterate habit of recording facts without studying them'. A.N. Wilson refers to this sloppy approach in a chapter devoted to Spencer in his 1999 book *God's Funeral*. Nobody could accuse Marx of talking out of his sock in this way: he would spend months reading through everything relevant to the subject in hand, and could spend hours tracking down references.

Marx's tomb did not always face Herbert Spencer's. The bodies of Karl, Jenny, their grandson Harry and their faithful Lenchen were moved to their current location in 1956. Their original grave had been rather modest: in 1956, a tomb designed by the communist sculptor Laurence Bradshaw was added. The original marble slab from the old grave was set into the front of the new memorial, which is topped by Bradshaw's bronze bust of Marx.

Like at least two of the Marx London memorial plaques, Marx's tomb has been vandalised. In 1960 Nazi symbols and words in German were painted on it, and in the nineteen-seventies there were even two attempts to blow it up. In 2019 somebody tried to smash the original memorial slab, and in the same year the tomb was daubed with slogans in red paint, declaring, among other things, that the tomb was a memorial to the 'bolshevik holocaust' and that Marx himself was the 'architect of genocide'.

In 1956, when the new tomb was unveiled, the ashes of the Marxes' youngest daughter Eleanor were added to the remains of her parents, her little nephew Harry and her beloved Lenchen. For years they had been stored at the Marx Memorial Library on Clerkenwell Green, which had been founded in a grand eighteenth century building in 1933. Before '33, the house had been used as the headquarters of the Twentieth Century Press, publishers of *Justice*, a left-wing weekly that ran articles by, among others, William Morris, Edward Aveling and the Russian anarchist Peter Kropotkin. Seventeen editions of Lenin's revolutionary paper *Iskra* were also published from here. The Marx Memorial Library remains an important resource for students of Marx, Marxism and associated subjects.

Like her sister Laura, Eleanor may also have killed herself, though Rachel Harris and others have speculated that her death from poisoning by cyanide may have been murder. She died at her house at number seven Jews Walk in the London suburb of Sydenham at the end of March 1898, at the age of forty-three. She shared the house, nick-named the Den, with her lover Edward Aveling. As Harris points out, and as friends of Eleanor realised at the time, accounts of how and when the poison was procured from the local chemist, and where Aveling was at the time of Eleanor's death, simply do not line up. Certainly Aveling inherited money on Eleanor's death, but he hardly had time to enjoy it: the man Marx's youngest daughter had met under the dome of the British Museum reading room died on the second of August 1898.

Marx's tomb at Highgate (John Armagh)

## Useful Addresses and Contacts

The British Museum
Great Russell St
London
WC1B 3DG

www.britishmuseum.org

The British Library
96 Euston Rd
London
NW1 2DB

www.bl.uk

The Museum Tavern
49 Great Russell Street
Bloomsbury
London
WC1B 3BA

www.greeneking-pubs.co.uk/pubs/greater-london/museum-tavern

B@1 (formerly the Red Lion)
20 Great Windmill Street
London
W1D 7LA

beatone.co.uk

4 Anderson Street
London
SW3 3LU

1 Leicester Street (formerly the German Hotel)
London
WC2H 7BL

Sola
64 Dean Street
London
W1D 4QQ

www.solasoho.com

Quo Vadis
26-29 Dean Street
Soho
London
W1D 3LL

www.quovadissoho.co.uk

46 Grafton Terrace (formerly # 9)
Belsize Park
London
NW5 4HY

22 Regent's Park Road
London
NW1 7TX

Highgate Cemetery
Swain's Lane
London
N6 6PJ

https://highgatecemetery.org

Marx Memorial Library & Workers' School
37a Clerkenwell Green
London

EC1R 0DU

https://www.marx-memorial-library.org.uk

# Select Bibliography

Aveling, Edward: *The Students' Marx*, George Allen & Unwin, 1891
Barker, Felix: *Highgate Cemetery: Victorian Valhalla*, John Murray, 1984
Beerbohm, Max: *Seven Men*, Heinemann, 1919
Berlin, Isaiah: *Karl Marx*, Oxford, 1949
Brandon, David: *London and the Victorian Railway*, Amberley, 2010
Briggs, Asa and Callow, John: *Marx in London*, Lawrence and Wishart, 2008
Bright, John: *Selected Speeches*, Dent, 1914
Brown, Siobhan: *A Rebel's Guide to Eleanor Marx*, Bookmarks, 2015
Cardwell, J.H.: *Men and Women of Soho*, Truslove and Hanson, 1903
Carlyle, Thomas: *Chartism*, Belford, Clarke & Co., 1890
Carver, Terrell: *Engels*, Oxford, 1981
Caygill, Marjorie: *The British Museum Reading Room*, BM, 2000
Cervantes, Miguel de: *Don Quixote*, Bohn, 1853
Chesterton, G.K.: *The Man Who Was Thursday*, Arrowsmith, 1912
Collins, Henry and Abramsky, Chimen: *Karl Marx and the British Labour Movement*, Macmillan, 1965
Conrad, Joseph: *The Secret Agent*, Penguin, 1963
Curl, James Stevens: *The Victorian Celebration of Death*, Sutton, 2000
Darwin, Charles: *On the Origin of Species*, Ward Lock, 1911
Dickens, Charles: *David Copperfield*, Dent, 1893
Disraeli, Benjamin: *Sybil*, Routledge, 1862
du Maurier, George: *Trilby*. Bell, 1896
Eagleton, Terry: *Why Marx Was Right*, Yale, 2018
Eliot, George: *Middlemarch*, Blackwood, 1891
Fedoseyev, P.N. et al: *Karl Marx*, Progress, 1973
Gonzalez, Mike: *A Rebel's Guide to Marx*, Bookmarks, 2006
Grossmith, George and Weedon: *The Diary of a Nobody*, Arrowsmith, 1919

Hunt, Tristram: *The Frock-Coated Communist: The Revolutionary Life of Frederick Engels*, Allen Lane, 2009
Institute of Marxism-Leninism of the CC, CPSU: *Reminiscences of Marx and Engels*, Foreign Languages Publishing House, 1957
Kingsford, P.W.: *Victorian Railwaymen*, Frank Cass, 1970
Liebknecht, Karl Marx: *Biographical Memoirs*, Journeyman Press, 1975
Lodge, David: *The British Museum is Falling Down*, Penguin, 1989
London, Jack: *People of the Abyss*, Cambridge, 2013
Maccoby, S: *English Radicalism 1832-1852*, Allen & Unwin, 1935
May, Trevor: *The Victorian Railway Worker*, Shire, 2008
McLellan, David: *Karl Marx, a Biography*, Palgrave, 2006
Moore, Alan and Lloyd, David: *V for Vendetta*, DC Comics, 1990
Nightingale, Florence: *Cassandra*, Feminist Press, 1979
Parsons, Gerald (ed.): *Religion in Victorian Britain: I: Traditions*, Manchester University Press, 1988
Payne, Robert: *The Unknown Karl Marx*, New York University Press, 1971
Picard, Liza: *Victorian London*, Weidenfeld & Nicolson, 2005
Shafer, David A: *The Paris Commune*, Palgrave, 2005
Spencer, Herbert: *Social Statics*, Appleton, 1897
Stevenson, Robert Louis: *The Dynamiter*, Longmans, 1903
Thomas, Paul: *Karl Marx*, Reaktion, 2012
Timbs, John: *Curiosities of London*, Virtue, 1828
Trollope, Anthony: *The Warden*, Oxford, 1952
Weitling, Wilhelm: *Garantien der Harmonie und Freiheit*, Vivis, 1842
Wells, H.G.: *The Time Machine and Other Works*, Reprint Society, 1945
Wheen, Francis: *Karl Marx*, Fourth Estate, 2000
Wilson, A.N.: *God's Funeral*, John Murray, 1999
Woolf, Virginia: *Jacob's Room*, Hogarth, 1922

Books by Karl Marx

*Capital, Volume 1*, Penguin, 2004
*The Cologne Communist Trial*, International, 1971
*Contribution to the Critique of Political Economy*, Progress, 1977
Fischer, Ernst (ed.): *Marx in His Own Words*, Pelican, 1973
*Herr Vogt*, Petsch, 1860

By Marx and Engels

*Articles on Britain*, Progress, 1971
*The Communist Manifesto*, Penguin, 2004

Feuer, Lewis S.: *Marx and Engels: Basic Writings on Politics and Philosophy*, Fontana, 1969
*Marx & Engels on Religion*, Schocken, 1964

For more Langley Press books, please visit our website at
www.langleypress.co.uk